this creative life

A Handbook for Writers

sara zarr

this creative life

contents

introduction

I often tell my students that they're the hosts of their books and stories, and may want to consider starting off their work with a mindset of hospitality. Let readers know where they are in time and space, I tell them. Introduce them to whoever is in the room.

In that spirit, I'll start by saying I'm the author of ten books and I've been writing for over twenty-five years, which is half my life. I've been a published author for over fifteen of those years, a podcast host for nearly ten, and a teacher, speaker, and coach throughout it all.

In those years of speaking at conferences, working with students, and talking to other writers on my podcast, This Creative Life, certain recurring themes keep coming up. They can be loosely clustered around two things: writing, and the business of writing. That is, fear and uncertainty around the act of writing, and fear and uncertainty about the business of being a published author or working writer. I'll be addressing both in this book.

For me, writing and sharing the writing (via the various tentacles of platforms and industry) are intimately connected. I've always written with the intent to publish, and the publishing business always pushes me back toward the perhaps unanswerable questions of how do we do this, why do we do this, and what even *is* the vague "this" that includes but is not limited to: the longing to tell stories; learning to accept our various character flaws and work habits so we can make progress in spite of ourselves; seeing ourselves as writers, even when there's no apparent evidence to back that identity up; and, once we do embrace that identity, keeping it from swallowing our lives in such a way that when we're not writing or success is not at hand, we don't experience the complete annihilation of our very selves.

Furthermore, how do we find a place in the publishing world, a place that feels like it's cooperating with our work and not scraping us dry? And if we can't do that, how do we make our own space for the writing, revising, and sharing of our stories?

My interest in these questions and my search for answers are what led me to start my podcast back in 2012, and is the compelling force behind this book. This is also the first book I've written in over fifteen years that does not come via a traditional publishing contract. That's opened up a whole new landscape of possibility and challenged my previously-held notions about self-publishing.

Taking this detour from the traditional path has been fun but also harrowing. With only my self-imposed deadline and the public promise of a release date to answer to, it's been tempting to tinker with the content of this book forever. Each question led to new topics; each new topic led to further questions. And without anyone but me to tell me when it was finished, there was a very real temptation to keep tinkering with it forever and not get around to the publishing part.

It would be an impossible and wrongheaded task to try to craft the perfect final word on every topic and question around writing that interests me. Even if I were able to capture everything I think about writing *now*, I would no doubt soon have new thoughts and want to say more about certain subjects, less about others.

But that's the thing about being a writer and being a person: we're always learning, changing, and adjusting our goals and our expectations. We get disenchanted and move on to something else. We drain one well and need to dig another. And yet, I think and hope that with this little book, I've been able to put together a fairly complete representation of the most important things I've learned or I suspect—so far—based on my experiences and the hundreds of hours I've spent talking to others at all stages of living a writing life.

The chapters herein range from brief reflections to deeper dives. They're organized broadly into three sections:

- The Writing Life (writing as a calling, identity, and way of seeing the world)
- Life at the Corner of Art & Commerce (writing for publication and the particular challenges therein)
- The Internal Arc (writing as a lifelong project)

If you've listened to the podcast, some of these topics and the way I approach them will be familiar. Nothing in this book ties directly or specifically to podcast episodes—I didn't want to hold guests to being quoted in print forever just because they may have agreed to be on a podcast once upon a time. You'll detect the recurring themes, though. And if you've never heard a single episode of the podcast, don't worry! This book is a philosophical companion to it, but it also stands alone. You don't need to be familiar with the podcast to get as much out of the book as those who have listened to every episode multiple times.

However you come to it, I hope you find something in these pages that feels like it was written just for you. It was.

disclaiming

Writing about writing often feels like a suspect enterprise.

For one thing, it can fall under the category of "self-help" or maybe "inspiration," and that makes me uneasy. I like being inspired and I've read some pretty good self-help books over the years, but I'm extremely wary of a particular kind of inspiration that doesn't acknowledge complexity and hardship, and a kind of self-help that is based on an equation of time + effort + method = the outcome you want. Systems for success, formulas for plots, templates for working the publishing system, or anything else that promises to make writing easy and success a guarantee mostly exist to take advantage of people's dreams.

For another thing, do even the most experienced writers really *know* what happens in those mysterious moments when an idea becomes language, characters come alive, plot problems get solved? Likewise on the career front, I don't think any writer *truly knows* how they got where they are. I suspect that if we could see into the Matrix, we'd discover there's a lot more luck and chaos involved in any success story than we like to think.

So I'm not making any claims in this book that if you do what I did, it will all work out for you as far as being published. I also know that writing is not a Couch to 10k endeavor, and you can't build a writing life and maybe a career on a foundation of productivity hacks and plot templates.

A writing life is more like walking a labyrinth. I mean that partly in the mythological sense—Daedalus building an intricate and disorienting structure to contain the Minotaur, so complicated that he can barely find his own way out. Writing can definitely feel like that. But I mostly mean labyrinth in the way religious mystics and contemplatives do. It's a pathway that looks like a maze, but it isn't. There are no dead ends; no one is trying to trap you. There also aren't shortcuts. It's a physical experience that exists in time and space, and the only way through it is through it, one foot in front of the other. Writing is like that, too.

I do think we can learn from other writers who have walked that path enough times to build up sound experience with regards to the craft of it, as well on the battle lines of getting out of your own way. I know I have, and at the end of this book there's a list of just a few resources that I find credible and useful.

If writing a book about writing is a suspect enterprise, reading them can be, too.

I say this because sometimes—*some*times—we do it to avoid actually writing. We do it because we *are* straining to find that one magical piece of information that will unlock all the doors. We do it because we want to feel like writers while also delaying the work of getting our own words down. Reading about writing can be busy-work or procrastination or resistance.

To be clear, I indulge in all of this behavior regularly.

But most of the time when I pick up one of my favorite books about writing or when I pick up one of the volumes of *The Paris Review* interviews I have on my shelf or click through links to read what others writers are saying this week, I'm not looking for answers so much as company. I'm not looking for the right way so much as mentorship from people who have already been through the territory I'm entering for the first time, or entering again with the knowledge that it's hard *every* time.

Most of all, I'm looking for reassurance that I'm not alone in feeling bad about my writing, feeling discouraged, feeling lost or confused or inadequate or anxious or any of the other variations of self-doubt that come up. That these feelings are not signs that I shouldn't keep going, that I shouldn't keep showing up. I'm looking for reminders that it's all just part of the deal.

I hope that in these pages, I can be that reminder and reassurance for you.

i. the writing life

1 /
the writing life defined for our purposes

I BELIEVE in a thing called "the writing life."

I believe writers are summoned (however you interpret that word) to a different way of seeing and inhabiting the world, a world of ideas and the cultivation of an inner life that comes through reading, contemplation, self-examination, curiosity, attention, and long stretches of quiet, or—more realistically—ongoing, sincere attempts at these things.

Maybe a better phrase for all of that is "the life of the mind," since it's available to anyone whether they write or not. It's just that writers have the additional step of processing and responding to all this inner work through the act of writing and, possibly, sharing the results—in fiction or nonfiction, books or scripts, poetry or prose, long-form or short form.

The life of the mind or the writing life doesn't depend on being a published or professional writer. It exists inside and outside and alongside and through day jobs, parenting, and any other context in which we find ourselves. It's about paying attention to the world and the people in it and committing time for our thoughts so we can make connections and dredge up (or gently excavate) whatever is going on in our less-conscious minds.

Basically, the writing life is active resistance to the hustle, the grind, the cycling through apps in hopes of finding something to make us feel momentarily okay, the avalanche of information, the instant judgments and reactions, the all-or-nothing and immediate-gratification-ness of the modern world.

Not every writer believes in all this or frames their work this way. Some writers think such talk is precious nonsense and favor the "it's a job, not a lifestyle" approach. I appreciate that pragmatic point of view, and sometimes thinking that way helps me get done what needs doing.

Ultimately, though, I want something more from it, and I think it has more to give than just being another job (though it can be that, too). For me, the writing life involves slowing down, going deep, being curious, paying attention, thinking through. It's a framework for living. It's both an invitation and a limitation calling me to say yes to some things I might want to resist and no to other things that tempt me.

Everything in this book comes down to these beliefs. That though "being a writer" is not the same thing as writing, the identity of "writer" is a real thing, a way of life, and an act of creation in itself. And no matter the practical limitations of our circumstances, if we approach it with sustainability in mind, we can make something of it for a lifetime.

2 /
the writer you are

PART of the foundation of a sustainable writing life is learning to accept the writer you are at any given point on your timeline. It took me a long time to realize how much my desire to be a different writer was keeping me from . . . you know, *writing*.

I've always wanted to be one of those writers who pops out of bed in the morning, hits the shower, makes a cup of coffee, and goes straight to the desk to dive into the work. Someone who wakes up and goes to bed with their enthusiasm for their work-in-progress intact, yet at the same time can hold it lightly enough that anxiety and perfectionism don't come for them in the wee hours (or all the hours). I want to be the professional working writer off to dig metaphorical ditches without any dithering. At quittin' time, that writer sits down with a well-deserved cocktail and some lively conversation or a good book.

Or I want to be the one who writes in a fever-dream,

taking dictation from characters and losing track of time for hours, maybe days, walking on clouds of inspiration and forgetting to eat and bathe until I emerge with a finished story and say, "I have no idea where that came from," and then get it published—lucratively!—with ease. The only notes from my editor are, "No changes!" and "Brilliant!" and "You did it again, Zarr!"

Heck, I'd even like to be the one who sets a modest daily goal—nothing outrageous—and gets it done consistently and without too much angst. The one with steady output and no drama.

Alas, I am none of those writers.

The truth is that writing has always been very difficult for me. It's always been something I have to fight for, be stubborn about, claw my way into. That's true both in terms of the process of getting it done and the process of making it good.

From the outset, I struggled to understand that I wanted to be a writer and that I was allowed to try. I was secretive and nervous about the whole endeavor. The decade-long path I started on a couple of years *after* college, when I finally admitted I wanted to at least give it a shot, was cobbled together out of focused reading, bad writing, researching, lurking, listening. I kept it up month after month and year after year, swinging precariously on vines of wishes and hopes until I found the next tree to hang onto.

I read books like the ones I wanted to write and was determined to write one through to the end. I learned everything I could about the business of writing and publishing. I lurked and loitered anywhere there might be writers who knew more than I did, and I listened. Also in play: desperation, sheer force of will, and—at times— the fury of having something to prove.

Trust me when I say that during this apprenticeship, I was not an undiscovered genius. For the majority of those years, there was very little indication that in the following decade I'd break through and find a level of success to be proud of. And still, it's common for me to feel as if I'm only hanging onto all of it by the very tips of my fingernails. Or freefalling until I can catch the next branch or toe-hold.

I don't know what my career or writing life looks like from the outside. Maybe it's surprising to hear that it feels this hard. Or maybe it's not, since I've always tried to be transparent. To a point. There's definitely a part of the author self-branding thing that means most public writers find it advantageous try to appear as successful as possible. This is the age of influence, after all, and it is not an exaggeration to say that appearing successful is almost as good as *being* successful and can even lead to success.

So there's an understandable fear around saying your latest book isn't selling, or you didn't get invited to the thing, or you're feeling scared about what might lie ahead. There's a reluctance to detail the ways a work-in-progress is breaking you, confounding you, getting away from you. That you fear, as I do with every single book, that this time you won't be able to do it. No one wants to look like a failure or even express *feeling* like a failure, and then become a self-fulfilling prophecy. Though I strive for honesty, I've been selective at times about exactly which truths to share.

My point here is: you can't really know how other people experience the writing process or a writing career. Maybe those idealized versions of writers that I wish I could emulate don't exist. Even if they do, there are reasons they'll never be me. Alcohol isn't great with my brain chemistry, no matter how well-deserved a cocktail might be, and my cat isn't big on lively conversation. I can't be the intense, lose-myself writer because I need calm routines and emotional balance. I've got a chronic disease that requires a lot of attention; if I lived on a cloud of inspiration and forgot to take my medication, I'd end up in the hospital. Steady output with no angst would probably be good, but it hasn't happened in any sustained way in twenty-five years of doing this, so I'm not counting on it.

I have to accept the writer I am and work with *her,* not some made-up version of what I want to be.

Maybe your idealized writer is the cool middle-aged woman in linen clothes and dangly earrings drinking tea from an earthenware mug, or the self-assured academic inspiring a roomful of undergrads, or the bearded baddie at the coffee shop whose fingers fly across the keyboard, or the cute nerd in the cat dress, or the one on fabulous retreats, or the squad that writes together by firepits with ice cold rosé and fresh blowouts.

It's good to have goals and a vision. And you can certainly put together the wardrobe and the beverages and the Apple products. You can try the hacks and habits and methods.

But it's my belief that you don't have a lot of control over whether writing comes easy for you or it's arduous, whether you are good at pumping yourself up or you fight self-doubt at every turn, whether you feel a sense of belonging or you are haunted by imposter syndrome. That's the stuff that cool glasses or job titles or even publishing success beyond your dreams don't tend to change. That's what can't be captured in a tweet or a pic.

You know how they say don't compare your first drafts to someone else's finished book?

Don't compare the interiority of your writing process to the exteriority of public writer personae.

We do grow and change and learn, we can learn and get better, we can work on the character traits that aren't helping us, we can acquire new habits and cultivate new ways of thinking.

But we all have to start by meeting ourselves where we are in the present moment.

3 /
claiming

You ARE SOMEBODY, and whether or not you reach your writing goals—now or at any point in the future or past or present—you do not need to constantly prove that, to yourself or to anyone else.

Do you write? Claim your right to call yourself *writer* right now.

If you need permission, give it to yourself.

If you need a space to read and write, go get one, even if it's in your car or the corner of a McDonald's (they do have free wi-fi, after all) or a diner booth (David Sedaris got his start journaling at IHOP while staying warm with free coffee refills), or a window seat at the public library.

If you need validation, cultivate it in a quiet place within.

I once knew a writer who put every nice thing anyone had said about them or their book into their email signature. Every time you got even a little email note from this person, there would be the reviews, quotes from anyone famous about the book, the time they were mentioned in a newspaper, a cool tweet from a hero. It was *all* there, all the time, and it took up half a screen.

I get it. There's absolutely nothing wrong with saving up nice things people have said about you and your work and tucking those words away in a special place in your consciousness, your "things about me" file that helps support the identity that feels like the truest you. Be proud! Highlight your accomplishments and share good news without apology.

But when I see myself (because of *course* I have done my versions of this) or anyone else making a very big point of ensuring that the world knows that we've gotten some stamp of approval from the external *them* so that we can perpetuate that approval from more of the *thems*, I just have this feeling it's not coming from a solid place of the truest self.

Who you are is more than what successes you have, what failures you experience, and what *they* have to say about it all. Who you are matters more than what you produce. Who you are is more than a quote from an anonymous Kirkus reviewer, or what your estranged dad said about your writing, or what your ex or former friend might think.

When I'm at my best, my writing identity comes from a deep and quiet place where the noise of approval and disapproval is a neutral background landscape more than a declaration of who I am. Conversely, the times I feel the worst about being a writer are when I'm looking for likes, fishing for approval, or otherwise in search of evidence that I'm *somebody*, because I've momentarily forgotten I already am.

If you acquire the regalia of being a published author, there's a place for showing that off. (After all, you want to make absolutely certain that any of your middle school bullies who might Google you know what's up.) Put it all on your website, stealthily add it to your Wikipedia page, drop those best-sellerdom status updates, get a tattoo. And yeah, put some choice quotes in your email signature if you want.

But remember, who you are is somewhere deeper than all that, somewhere permanent that can't be blown over by the fickle winds of other people's opinions. And you may need to do some work—therapy and/or self-help and/or conversations with trusted friends—to fully shed yourself of the need for external approval from *them*, where *them* is always a moving target.

And if the day comes that *you* are a *them* that other people look to for that hit of validation, remember that they may need you to remind them that they are someone, too.

If you write, you're a writer. The only permission you need is yours; the validation that matters most is the quiet kind that comes from within.

4 /
a defense of grandiosity

WHEN I FINISHED the very first draft of my very first novel, way back in the late 1990s, I *immediately* put it in the mail to a then well-known contest for first young adult novels. Then my husband and I went to an arcade on San Francisco's Pier 39 to celebrate and play air hockey.

I'd really made it! I'd finished my first novel, and it would surely knock the socks off the contest judges. The prize money would be mine and my career would—after one whole year of working at it—take off.

It will not surprise you to know that I eventually got a thin envelope containing a form letter thanking me for my submission, but I did not win. In fact, if I recall this correctly, there were *no* winners that year. Apparently, my book was worse than no book at all.

I felt extremely disappointed and even shocked by this. Had they really even *read* my book? Maybe my manuscript had gotten mixed up with someone else's.

Maybe it got lost in the mail. It was all deeply appalling, not to mention *suspicious*.

I can laugh about this now, but at the time I was genuinely crushed.

Similarly, a student of mine recently confessed grave disappointment at their book not winning a competition they'd entered. They referred to themself as a "dumb-dumb" with a "big head" and expressed other rueful thoughts about their belief that they were a contender.

Listen. We all have to have an at least slightly exaggerated or even grandiose idea about our own skills—especially when we're starting out—or else we'd never, ever put our writing out there.

The contest that decided a big empty space was preferable to my very first novel? It got me to finish a book-length work for the first time. My student's failed submission offered them practice at experiencing rejection, which (sorry to say) comes in useful at all stages of the writing life. You making a run at National Novel Writing Month and "only" finishing half the fifty-thousand-word goal? That's twenty-five thousand words you otherwise wouldn't have written in such a short time.

If we weren't overconfident in ourselves as new writers, we wouldn't query agents, stand up at open mics, or even sign up for classes (after all, isn't part of the reason we take classes to impress the teacher with how much we *don't* need their class?).

Chances are good that someday, you'll feel sheepish about your early (or not-so-early) delusions of grandeur.

But for now, use them to your advantage. Let unearned confidence be a temporary bridge for you until you've built your way to something more solid. The railings of this bridge are a robust sense of humor about yourself and a determined hunger to earn everything you may now have to fake.

5 /
identity & family of origin

LIKE IT OR NOT, we all have a family of origin.

We were born into some situation or other—good, bad, or neutral. And it probably comes with some *shit*. Some Family of Origin Shit.

By which I mean we were all raised by *some*one or some group of someones, and we all come out of that experience with messages about who we are and what we're about, what we're capable of and what we fear, what we're allowed to do, how high we're permitted to aim, how big we're allowed to dream and what the content of those dreams should be.

Some people come from an environment that helped them dream and try things. For them, failure was no big deal, and they were allowed to play at all sorts of interests and identities.

Others come from dire circumstances and deep dysfunction: poverty and other economic instability, addictive family systems, homes where love was withheld or transactional, places that weren't physically or emotionally safe, and other varieties of traumatic and abusive situations.

A lot of us are somewhere between those scenarios. Our families of origin have some degree of dysfunction, and are somewhere on the spectrum of a broad definition of functional. Along with some positive experiences, we have our wounds and scars. And we have a set of messages about who we are—including, perhaps, ideas about the word "creative" and how it applies to us.

Remember that word when it wasn't a noun or a corporate job? Once upon a time, it was an adjective, describing a person or a thing. Some of us heard that word in relation to our identity very early on, for better or for worse, depending on the values of our family and community.

In some families, to be creative was a good thing. It meant, *Wow, you're a person I find inspiring and interesting!* Or, *The stuff you come up with is so cool!*

In other families, it was a label used in opposition to something else. As in:

You're creative, but your brother is athletic.

You're not creative; you're a math whiz!

You may not have a lucrative career ahead but, hey, at least you're creative.

Worst of all for the kid struggling to be accepted, "creative" might have been code for *You're a weirdo* or *You're not like us* or *I don't understand you.*

On the other extreme, the word could be full of

expectations. You might come from a family that holds creativity and creative careers in the highest esteem. Maybe your grandmother was a writer, or your dad was first cello in a symphony, or your aunt is on Broadway, or you are the third sibling in a row to be working on a novel. To be creative in that kind of family means *You're one of us.* Or it could mean, *You're one of us, and that's great as long as you don't succeed more than Dad.* Or, *You're one of us but not as good at being one of us as your sister.*

My own life has involved a little of all of those things.

I've been the creative kid who liked to read and play make believe and draw and dance but never got picked for kickball. I've been the high school drama kid defined by what I wasn't: not athletic; not cool. *Creative.* In the little suburb where I spent high school, being "creative" in an externally visible way pretty much labeled you as a freak.

Yet I also come from a family where creative professions were sought after and respected. There are musicians and writers in my tree, some who did those things professionally for a time, some who wanted to but couldn't. Being well-read and "cultured" was a value. Despite our financial situation, my sister and I got music lessons, and we were in a ballet theater, thanks in part to the generosity of better-off relatives. My dad woke me up in the night to watch the late movie if it was a classic I should know. We checked out veritable towers of books from the library. Writers, actors, composers, poets, and musicians were admirable, and their works were part of what enriched life.

Still, it took me a long time to stake out that declaration for my*self*, that I was a writer or trying to be one, and I wanted to be one professionally. In retrospect, there was a lot going on that I wasn't completely conscious of. Both my parents had at one time had promising futures in the music world and could have made a nice life combining professorships with semi-professional music performance. Both were psychologically thwarted in their own ways, as well as by the practical realities of raising kids and trying to make ends meet.

If I risked an attempt, would I be thwarted, too? If I wasn't thwarted, would I somehow be punished? Along with everything else in my childhood, I was steeped in 1970s Jesus Movement Christianity, and even into my early adulthood I wasn't sure if it was okay to *want* to be creatively successful.

I couldn't quite put my finger on all of this. But I had the sense I was stepping outside the lines in prioritizing the attempt to make a creative dream into a reality, maybe even into a career.

And as it turned out, I wasn't imagining it.

The first time I shared with my estranged father that I was making a serious go at writing, he said, incredulous, "Have you ever even taken a class?" in the same tone you would use to say, "What makes *you* think you can do this?" And as I progressed in my quest and told him about getting an agent, he said, "I don't think I could ever bear to see a book by you on a shelf." He was intoxicated, and I should have known better than to ask why he would say this, but I did and he answered, "I'd be too jealous."

So there was a *reason* I had that vague and protective sense of wanting to be sure within myself about what I wanted and to have made some headway before I dared to share it with my family. It's really something when the things beneath the surface get directly stated! Maybe it's a kind of a gift, the opposite of being gaslit.

Throughout my years of knowing other published writers, I have learned that the outlines of my story are not unique. Funny stuff happens when you dare to stake out a claim in creative territory. People come out of the woodwork, resentments bubble up to the surface, the thwarted or deferred dreams of others come out sideways and gather into a cloud of *but I wanted that* hovering over already-complicated relationships.

To fully give yourself permission to go forward with your writing, you might need to think about the word and the identity "creative" and see if it has any baggage for you, any Family of Origin *shit*. Try to think about all the associations you have with that word, good or bad. What are the forces and experiences within that push or pull you toward or away from the identity of writer? When you think about writing and being a writer, do you feel held back in some vague way? Could silent (or not so silent) messages from people in your life be astir? Maybe it's a topic to journal on, if you like journaling, or bring up in therapy, if you do that. At least give it some thought.

And if your gut instinct is to keep your writing dreams and activities out of the family newsletter or friend reunion, listen to your gut. You don't need to tell anyone else what you're up to in order to make it real. Keep it close as long as you need to.

6 /
talent

IN THE LAST ten years or so, I've had a number of opportunities to lead workshops or do one-on-one critiques at conferences and in other settings. More than once, I've been pulled aside at some point by a participant and asked some version of, "Do I have *it*? Do you think I can make it? Do I have talent?"

They want me—*me*, who has only had the merest glimpse into their writing, *me* with my own tastes and preferences, *me* who showed very little promise when I first started writing—to give a pass or a fail to their dream, based on a highly suspect concept that we call *talent*.

Talent. Aptitude. Innate ability. The gift. The X factor. Star quality.

Whatever you call it, it's *so* beside the point.

I once heard artist and writer Barry Moser speak, and in this speech he said something about the idea of talent that has stuck with me for nearly twenty years. To wit:

"Talent is as common as house dust and as useless as tits on a boar."

It wasn't only the colorful language that made it memorable, but also the idea behind it. It immediately sounded right to me back then, and my experience in the years since has confirmed it.

Talent *is* common. Every writer I've ever worked with has at least a little. It might look like a knack for writing action scenes, a poet's gift for imagery, a deep understanding of human nature, a rich imagination, an innate sense of pace, a flair for bringing humor to the page, expertise at making readers cry, or enough of a few of these things to make their writing stand out from go.

But talent, like Moser said, is useless in and of itself. We've all met those writers who can do some or all of the above with a kind of natural ease that we'd metaphorically kill for, but they never manage to get anything finished or submitted. We've known (or have been) "talented" writers who self-sabotage, or can't focus the talent, or aren't willing to improve it. Without a consistent or even semi-consistent approach to work, persistence in the face of obstacles, dedication to the craft of whatever it is we're doing, mental and physical self-care practices that protect our writing, and patience in what can be a slow process, talent gets us nowhere.

This should be an encouragement to anyone who does not feel gifted by the gods in the talent department, or a warning to anyone who has been gifted in such a way but hasn't yet wrangled that gift. For me, it's mostly the former, because there are certain things about writing that I've always found a real struggle.

For example, coming up with the words.

I'm not kidding! Writing does not "pour out of me." Great sentences do not come naturally or easily. Knowing how to make an idea for a situation into a *plot* hurts my brain. I don't feel naturally talented and all the things I need to write novels. But I know I want to tell these stories in my head, that they matter to me, and they could matter to someone else if I try hard enough to pull them out. Persistence, dedication, and patience have helped me do that work, not whatever innate talent I may have.

Here's a little metaphor for anyone familiar with Texas Hold'em poker. If you've ever found yourself watching the World Series of Poker, ever watched any movies about poker, or played poker online, you were probably watching or playing Hold'em.

In Hold'em, each player is dealt two cards. Those are called your pocket cards or your hole cards, and those are private—no one else knows what you have. That's the hand you're dealt.

Then there are five cards dealt to the table. These are for everyone, and they come in three stages: the flop (three cards), the turn (one card), and the river (one last card). Everyone tries to come up with the best five-card hand they can out of these seven cards—the two pocket cards and the five table cards.

Let's say those pocket cards represent your innate talent at a given moment, and the table cards are everything else—the marketplace, the cultural zeitgeist, editors, agents, reviewers, and anything else about writing that's hard to predict or control.

And let's say you get dealt a pair of kings—a pocket pair of kings. Let's say a spade and a club. You seem to have a lot of natural talent and all you have to do is sit back and get ready to rake up your chips. After all, a high pocket pair is a hard hand to beat!

Or is it?

The flop comes and it's a 3-4-5 of hearts.

Now your kings aren't looking quite as great. Still strong, but the flop didn't help you and might have helped someone else. Imagine you're another player at the table and you've got a 2-7 of hearts that you almost folded before the flop. Your pocket hand is weak all on its own. But the table cards—the marketplace, the zeitgeist, etc.—are aligned for you, and suddenly you've got a flush, and a straight flush draw. That's hard to beat.

Depending on what comes on the turn and the river, either hand could still take the pot. The turn could be Oprah or Reese liking your book, the river could be going viral on TikTok, or a great NYT review or a movie option. You can't predict or control it. All you can do is play your hand.

This is where the importance of persistence comes in,

where the dedication to learning the craft of the game matters. Good players, the ones who make the World Series of Poker, have played enough hands and learned enough strategy and been consistent and persistent in the face of losses that they can play weak hands strategically, hope for luck to hit, or fold and move on to the next.

Because here's the thing: in poker and in writing, you get new hands all the time. The amount of talent you may or may not have isn't set in stone. It grows and changes with the time you put into your writing, the new information you take in, the learning you do, the various ideas for plots and stories you have.

And when you sense that your pocket cards *are* good —all that practice and failure and time have strengthened your hand—it can be really frustrating when you keep getting beat by how the table cards come down. That is, when the marketplace doesn't want what you're doing, or your work hasn't found the right agent or editor or opportunity, or luck hasn't otherwise lined up to go your way.

Yes, there is a time to walk away from the table.

In poker, when you're on a bad streak and you're just chasing losses and making desperate plays, it's called being "on tilt." You're exhausted, frustrated, and you start to hate the game. But you're caught up in the sunk-cost fallacy and think that if you just grit your teeth and hang in there, you'll recoup your losses. Your decision-making capacity is in the red; you've blown out your instincts.

That's a good time to get up and sit out a few hands, drink some water, take some breaths. Or it's time to go home and get some sleep and forget about the whole world of poker until the love of the game draws you back.

I've been there—in poker and in writing.

When I started out, I didn't have an undeniable talent. I got rejected a lot. I remember applying for a grant at one point and the comments I got back were along the lines of, "There's nothing special about this." No one was reading my writing and saying, *She's going to be a star!*

Then I wrote more, learned more, read more. I got better. I got an agent and a book I wrote made it to acquisitions. My pocket hand was looking strong. And then the table cards didn't go my way. It wasn't the right book at the right time. There was no deal, and eventually I left that agent.

The years after that were a roller-coaster of near hits and misses. I *knew* my game was getting better. I was improving my skills and honing my instincts. And I still couldn't win. I wasn't getting the calls; there was no sign of the "yes" I needed.

Around my seventh year at trying to get a novel published, I was fairly miserable. I hated books, writing, writers, publishing, and anything that reminded me of those things. I couldn't go into a book store. I couldn't deal with anyone else's good news. I rage-queried and hate-read.

I was on tilt.

And I had to walk away from writing and the attempt

to get published until I could come back to it rested and because I wanted to.

Finally, the strength of my hand lined up with the table cards. Right book, right agent, right editor, right publisher, right time, right luck. All told, it took about a decade to get to that.

I could have fallen prey to "I just don't have it" thinking; I could have decided to fold and leave the table years before that happened.

And, to be clear, I know that just because hanging in there worked for me, it's no guarantee it will work out that way for everyone. But I also know that "Am I talented?" is not the question to be asking, and it's especially not something to ask someone who has only a passing familiarity with your work. Don't give them that power.

The questions to ask are the ones only you can answer:

Am I dedicated? Am I willing? Am I patient?

Can I learn? Will I work? Do I care?

Do I love (or enjoy, or like) this enough to stay at the table even when the game isn't going my way?

7 /
giving & receiving feedback

MANY OF US start out in workshops or classes, reading each other's pieces and offering constructive criticism. If we haven't been in a formal workshop or class environment, we might find a writing community online or a writing partner with whom we share work in hopes of making it better. We may have done this as far back as in our high school or middle school English classes.

Even the most seasoned writers eventually need outside perspective and input on a given project. For professionals, feedback is built into the publishing process—we work with editors and copyeditors to get our work as close to our vision as we can. And I and most working writers I know still often call on writer friends to provide a fresh set of eyes at crucial points in the process.

When you're starting out, though, it takes more intent to get a helpful feedback loop going. First of all, you've got to find some sort of writing community, online or in-person. That can feel like a big project in itself. But once you've got that set of people in your orbit, it's not as simple as swapping pages and hoping for the best.

During the decade I was writing but not yet published, I collected a good deal of experience with writing groups in person, writing pals online, and workshops ranging from weekend Learning Annex stuff to weeklong intensives out of town. As a published author (and also a mentor and coach), I've continued to learn the best practices for giving feedback and getting it. Here's a distillation of that collected experience:

Be ready.

Are you ready to get feedback? Have you gotten as far on the piece as you can on your own? Do you have at least a general sense of your vision for the project?

If the answer to any of these things is no, you may not be ready to go out and solicit input. I can't tell you how many of my ideas have died on the vine because I exposed them to the elements too soon! If you haven't given your little seedling the unconditional love and care it needs to grow some roots, it's not going to stand up to even the most helpful critique. You'll barely even be able to decipher good advice from bad if you don't know yet yourself what you want the thing to be. So before you seek feedback, make sure the work can stand on its own legs—wobbly though they may be.

Choose wisely.

You've probably heard before that it's better to have no critique group than a bad one. I see no lie there. Who you invite into your process matters; there's got to be trust between you and the potential critique-giver. There are a couple of aspects to the trust issue:

The first is that the best writing is personal and involves the writer getting vulnerable in some way, and where there's vulnerability, there's the risk of getting hurt. I'm not a big fan of the "viciously tear the thing apart" school of feedback. I believe a good critique meets your writing halfway. That is, the person giving feedback takes some steps toward the work, even if it's not their preferred style of writing. Giving feedback isn't about "How would *I* do this," but about "How can I help them do what *they* want to do?" If you can't trust a person to read your work in good faith, meet it on its terms, and respect the vulnerability on the page, they're probably not the right choice.

Second, you want to trust that the person knows what they're talking about. You wouldn't ask your vegetarian friend to critique your short ribs. You would find a friend who's a short rib connoisseur, who can diagnose your seasonings, troubleshoot your technique, and appreciate everything you did right. Ideally, you find a fellow writer who understands and likes the kind of thing you're working on, and whose work or taste you respect.

Communicate expectations.

I vividly remember the very first time a fellow writer gave me feedback on some of my own pages. He offered, so I said yes, emailed the pages, and waited. When he sent them back, I opened up the document and saw my sentences crossed out and re-written, margin comments, my words moved all around into different order.

I was angry to the point of nausea. I felt violated!

The issue (as it so often is) was expectations. I thought I was going to get back a paragraph with a summary of a few strengths and a few things for me to work on. He thought he was doing a line edit.

Since then, I've learned to state clearly what I'm looking for in a particular round of feedback. For example: "Can you read this over and tell me if it makes sense overall? If not, where is it confusing?" Or, "I'm struggling with the relationship between these two characters. Can you read this section and tell me what you think?" Or even, "Please do a slash and burn on this; I am so lost."

Going in with clear expectations can save time, energy, and friendships! (Bonus tip: this is true about virtually everything in life.)

Ask questions (but don't argue).

Getting the feedback isn't necessarily the end of the communication. If there's something in the critique you're confused about, ask for clarification. If something opens up new questions about the work, ask those questions.

Non-defensive questions are great and reasonable; arguing is not. Sometimes you'll get feedback you want to argue with—you're only human. A reader might totally misunderstand your work or come up with potential solutions that you reject out of hand. That's okay. It could be that the work just isn't for them, and you don't need to go out of your way to convince them of anything. Or it could be they're pointing out a legit problem, but the solution they're suggesting is not right for you. Sometimes people we ask for critique can diagnose but not treat. Pay attention to the diagnosis. If it feels off to you, get a second opinion. Then you can work on figuring out a treatment approach.

In any case:

Say thank you.

Because I'm a published novelist who's been around a while, I get a fair number of requests for reads from strangers. Sometimes, if it's something short and sounds interesting and I have time, I say sure, and I read and send along my thoughts. And you would be surprised (or maybe you wouldn't) at how often someone fails to close the feedback loop with a simple thank you. My notes seem to go into a black hole and the person is never heard from again.

Whether the person giving your work a read is a

friend, stranger, acquaintance, classmate, or teacher, "thank you" is always appropriate. Even if it turns out the advice isn't helpful or you feel defensive or mad or any other of those human feelings, if a person took the time to engage with your work in good faith, say thanks.

Reciprocate.

While you're saying thanks, it's also good practice to offer to reciprocate. If you're getting a peer-to-peer critique, this is fairly straightforward. You read my stuff, I read yours, we try to give each other helpful feedback, and everyone's happy. Yay!

If you've asked a writer who's a lot farther along on the path than you to give feedback, and they do it, it may not feel right to offer to give them feedback next time they're looking. In that case, you can pay it forward when you've got some experience and a newer writer comes along and needs some perspective on their work.

And remember—when you're asked to give feedback, you can model the "communicate expectations" step of this process. Ask, "What kind of feedback are you looking for on this draft? Anything in particular? Or should I just dive in and pull no punches?"

Be true to your vision.

Feedback is just feedback. Some of it will be helpful. Some of it will miss the mark. Some of it will help you diagnose but not cure. Some of it will say more about the reader than about your writing. Some of it will be pure trash! It happens.

This all brings us back to the very first step: be ready. You want to be solid enough in your vision to be able to recognize the good stuff and put it to work for you. With practice, you'll develop your confidence and your gut so that you know when a point of critique is right. It will resonate and kick your problem-solving muscles into gear and feel exciting. And when it's not right, you'll be able to non-defensively say "thank you" and leave it on the table.

8 /
attention &
curiosity

WHAT TRAITS DO you need to be a writer?

Imagination helps. A basic grasp of how stories work is good, as is a decent vocabulary. You can absorb those things simply by being a reader. If you want to be a long-form writer, tolerance for delayed gratification and the ability to manage a long-term project are handy, but if you don't naturally have those skills, they can be learned. So can self-editing.

That's all a good starting point. Learn how plots work, think up characters and stories, and put in the time. Write to the end of a draft; make it better.

But if you want your work to go deeper and higher, to dig in and transcend, there are two habits that will keep giving back to you if you cultivate them: curiosity and attention.

If you're a writer or writing-inclined person, you're probably already familiar with feelings of acute or painful self-awareness. You probably have an urge to analyze or overanalyze your thoughts and actions and relationships. You see your inner life as a rich (or frightening, or puzzling) field of exploration. You're curious about yourself and what's going on inside you.

The curiosity turns outward, too. You might love cult podcasts or true crime or reality TV. You might have a taste for gossip. Not in the sense of being cruel or backbiting, but in wanting to know things like: What the heck happened between those people? Who said what and how did they say it? Did they really? What was the reaction? Why would they do that? What were they thinking?

Maybe you love nothing more than going down a Wikipedia rabbit hole for hours on end, or binge-watching documentaries, or reading nonfiction. However it expresses itself, you are in some way curious about yourself, others, and how the world works.

Attention is the companion of curiosity. Without it, curiosity is merely an abstract that doesn't go anywhere. That is, you can't stop at, "Hmm, I wonder why that person did that strange thing," or, "I wonder why I can't just get along with my brother," and then carry on as before. A writer's curiosity should lead to investigation and observation, and deep attention to your findings.

That being said, not every point of curiosity will lead to deeper deliberation. While we may have endless curiosity, attention is a finite resource. We don't have a limitless ability to notice all the things, or limitless time to give to all that noticing. Quite literally, "paying" attention costs us. Once we've paid our attention, there are no refunds. The meme "I'll never get that hour of my life back" is literal truth. As someone who can be fascinated by almost *anything* and *anyone*, it's a hard truth to accept. It gets a little easier as I've gotten older and more profoundly in touch with my numbered days.

Part of my "life of the mind" discipline is to manage my attention as the finite resource it is. Living through the pandemic and the politics of the last five or so years has been real test of this. Information and content just keep coming in a continuous tsunami. I've watched hours and days and weeks of my attention fall through my fingers at an incredible rate. I've also been able to draw a direct line from what I give my attention to, to how I feel. How much fear and anxiety I have, how much hope and joy there's room for, how much capacity I have to write novels and grow stories. With the thousands of bits of news and information I was constantly letting in, there wasn't a whole lot of attention left to spend on writing and reading. My curiosity, too, got stunted by the news-reaction-news-reaction cycle, and too much time watching a feed of other people's neatly summed-up opinions on complicated issues.

An individual's capacity for attention varies, of course. Some people seem to have the ability to jump from news to writing to celebrity gossip, to what's happening on their favorite show, to making podcast recommendations, to sharing a funny story, to making a profound point about trauma. If I ever had that capacity,

I don't now. Probably most people don't. People who feel they do might be wrong. And who knows, maybe they lie awake at night anxious, too.

The bottom line is: pay attention to your attention. It's a huge part of what makes up our writing voice and what leads us to the topics and characters and questions that draw us toward one idea over another. Watch for recurring themes in your attention. Notice what you're drawn to, and have curiosity about why. Why this and not that? Why now? Consider keeping a commonplace book or journal or some digital collection of what you pay attention to. It all makes a kind of mental collage that can come together in a book idea, a writing style, or a career plan.

9 /
the people business

SPEAKING OF ATTENTION AND CURIOSITY, it's worthwhile to spend much of it on the inner workings of human nature. Why are we the way we are? What makes us tick? What makes us do bad things, act against our own best interest, make choices out of line with our purported beliefs?

I firmly believe that to be a writer is to be in the business of people. We write *about* people (or robots or animals, but even those are usually stand-ins for humans in a story), and we write *for* people. Novels, poetry, short fiction, creative nonfiction, memoir . . . they all involve being human.

Listen to writer-director Tony Gilroy when he says:

"The quality of your writing is absolutely capped at your understanding of human behavior. You'll never write above what you know about people." [1]

Gilroy is known mostly for the Jason Bourne movies, *Michael Clayton*, and *Rogue One: A Star Wars Story*.

I like those movies. But I *love* that quote and I think it's true.

Human behavior is odd and people can never be fully understood, but writers need to try. It starts with working on understanding ourselves as much as possible. Develop curiosity about yourself and why you do the things you do. What makes you want to hide? What impels you to lash out? Read self-help books about your particular issues. Therapy may be in the cards. If you want to go farther, take personality type tests (like the Enneagram, the MBTI, Core Strengths, etc.) and read up on your results.

Try not to be satisfied with a surface-level relationship with who you are, or with reacting and judging when someone does something you don't understand. Dig in, and watch how it pays off in the depth of your writing and, hopefully, your emotional health.

---

1. http://static.bafta.org/files/tony-gilroy-lecture-transcript-2058.pdf

10 /
characteristics of a
sustainable writing
life

THERE'S no real endgame in a creative life. While we certainly have goals we want to reach and milestones we want to hit and maybe a career bucket list, there's no ultimate arrival.

I used to think that publication was the point. I thought that once I hit that goal of my name on a book published by a New York publisher, I wouldn't want anything else. I'd *know* I'd arrived and everything after that would just be . . . extra.

But then I wanted good sales. I wanted better reviews. I wanted a bunch of fans. One book felt like nothing. I wanted a body of work that would be . . . five books. No, ten. Well okay, fifteen. Make it twenty. I wanted certain conference invitations and networking connections. I've gotten some of these things and have hit ten books. I've had some awards recognition. I even got to see a movie made from one of my books.

Those are great career milestones, and I'm grateful

for them. Yet I don't feel like any of those things have brought me closer to a sense of being done. I think that's because people in creative careers don't tend to fantasize about being able to quit or retire. There's generally no "One more book, three more years with my nose to the grindstone of bringing stories to life, and then I can finally quit and work on my golf game."

Admittedly I have at times daydreamed about getting off the publishing treadmill, but that's not the same thing as "quitting writing." Generally speaking, we're doing this for life. And if you're working in long-form writing, any given project can take years. Even good short-form writing can involve months of research and revision. Maybe more.

Without instant gratification or a discernible finish line, sustainability becomes an important consideration. How do we do this for the long term—over years and years, over a lifetime—and not flame out?

Sustainability in a writing life is going to be a little different for everyone. I've been doing this about half my life now, and these are some of the key characteristics of a sustainable writing life that have been true for me and so many writers I've talked to:

It's engaging.

For me to even want to get out of bed in the morning and write, the work first and foremost has to be personally engaging. It has to tap into something deep within that matters to me, or interests me, or tickles my curiosity, or asks me a question. I want it to bring me closer to my truest self. I want it to make me feel part of the world. I need it to expand me, not reduce me to my screens and word counts.

Does that sound a little romanticized? It is. What I describe here is my ideal. The reality often feels pretty different. I can forget why I'm doing what I'm doing and how I ever thought it was a good idea. I think those are pretty common feelings, especially if you have the kind of brain I do and struggle with focus, boredom, and distraction. It's normal to want to get out of a task once it becomes difficult. That can be overcome, though, if you're working on something that you know you want to finish.

If I *ever* found a project engaging, I know I can re-engage. But I can't write something I don't care about. Some writers can, and to pay the bills, they do. I've tried that, and I'd rather go out and do grocery delivery gigs or sell my plasma than spend one more minute of my life trying to write a good sentence about something I can't personally engage with.

It invites company.

A lot of writers are introverts. In order to thrive, we desperately need our alone time. It doesn't mean we don't enjoy being with other people, it just means that socializing is draining for us and takes preparation and recovery. But we do need other people. And writers need a specific category of "other people" in addition to family and friends.

Writers need a community of writers.

These could be writers that write the same kind of stuff that you do, or they could be writing in an entirely different genre or category. It doesn't matter. It only matters that they really get it when it comes to the particular joys and struggles and desires that writers experience. Maybe you find just one person who clicks; maybe you find a dozen. The size of your circle doesn't matter, only that you have one.

Seek mentorship. You may find mentorship among your writing circle, or outside of it. A mentor could be a paid professional, or the person sitting next to you at a conference who has figured out how to enlist her partner or kids in supporting her creative life. Maybe someone who is years younger than you, with far less experience, has a certain calmness or wisdom you wish you had. Or they're an exemplar of discipline.

You may find mentorship from people you can never meet or interact with directly. They may even be dead! Read biographies of writers whose work moves you. Follow careers from a distance. Pay attention; you never know in what unconventional forms mentorship may appear. Try to lead a mentored life when it comes to your writing, and be open to possibility as various people come into it.

That said, do have some discernment. Be a little

choosy. A hundred people you don't really know on Twitter are not the same thing as an inner circle of trusted peers. Look for comrades who you can build trust with, who see who you are with compassion and good humor, and who can keep confidences.

It knows when to send company away.

Mentors and peers are wonderful, important, and valuable. But ultimately this is about you, and when it comes down to the moment of getting your writing done, no one can do it for you. *You* have to choose which critiques to take, what career advice to heed, which way your characters will turn, and the stories you want to tell.

Some unpublished writers are surprised to learn that even our editors don't just tell writers what to do. They offer experienced guidance and suggestions, but the final word generally goes to the writer. This makes it even more important to know when to "close the door," as Stephen King puts it, and develop an inner compass, a kind of divining rod that you can rely on when it's just you and the work.

If you're in a stage of your writing life where you're in critique groups or school but you haven't been published, this is an instinct that can take time to sharpen. There's such a thing as too much feedback, and if you find yourself stuck in a loop of reacting to feedback and trying to "fix" your book to satisfy one person only to dissatisfy the next, it's time to step back, close that door, and listen to your gut. What's the book *you* want to write, the story *you* want to tell in the way only *you* can tell it? It's okay to not have a clear answer. But you need to be alone with the questions for a while before you invite that company back in.

It's faith-based.

I'm not talking here about religious faith. But a sustainable writing life takes a tremendous amount of faith in *something*, even if that something is only itself.

Before you're published, if that's your goal, there is so little tangible evidence that what you're doing matters, that anyone cares, that you can and will grow and improve, that someone other than you will understand and want what you have to offer.

Even in the midst of a career as a published writer, there are moments (or years, or seasons) where all practical signs point to NO. There are times for me when there's no demand for what I do. Seasons when not a single person is clamoring for my next book, my inbox is quiet, my phone ain't ringing.

That's when faith is the only thing that keeps me working. Faith that if I show up to the page and give my attention and curiosity, something will happen. Faith that all the stories haven't been used up already by other writers. Faith that I've finished manuscripts before (about fifteen of them), and I can do it again.

And to get a little woo-woo, I have some faith in the

generosity of the universe, in the material all around me, and that imagination is not a finite resource. I like how Dorothy Sayers puts it:

"The amount of matter in the universe is limited . . . But no such limitation of numbers applies to the creation of works of art. The poet is not obligated, as it were, to destroy the material of a Hamlet in order to create a Falstaff, as a carpenter must destroy a tree-form to create a table-form. The components of the material world are fixed; those of the world of imagination increase by a continuous and irreversible process, without any destruction or rearrangement of what went before."

I have faith in that.

It gives back.

A sustainable creative life gives back to you, and it gives back to others.

As you're engaged with your work and with the world and with other people, and rooted in some kind of faith in what you're doing, you'll probably be a better person. You'll probably be a better partner, parent, friend, co-worker, or sibling because for some amount of time, for some number of days a week, you're answering that call to write.

Nothing makes me crankier, meaner, and more full of self-loathing than when I've gone extended periods of time without writing even though I know it's what I want to do and what I'm meant to be doing. I'm like a dog who hasn't been played with enough, or a bird who hasn't gotten to sing, or a car that's been sitting in a garage for so long that I can only belch out toxic fumes and scary noises.

I've said that if you write, you're a writer. The reverse is also true: if you're a writer, you need to write. Even if you're not achieving certain career or artistic markers on your schedule, you'll be self-actualized or in the process of self-actualizing, and that's what helps equip you to give back to the world in a variety of ways. Above, I mentioned the importance of seeking out mentorship. It's just as important to *be* a mentor when the time is right, and that's a great way to give back, whether you are mentoring in the realm of writing or in other realms your life and experiences touch.

11 /
obstacles to a sustainable writing life

JUST AS THERE are characteristics of a sustainable writing life, there are also obstacles to it. I'm not talking about the challenges of *writing* itself, but the habitual behaviors and mindsets that generally make a writing life or life of the mind harder, sadder, and more elusive than it needs to be.

Disenchantment.

I think of this as the opposite of engagement, and it's a common affliction of adulthood.

You can think of it as cynicism or disillusionment, being jaded or hardened by the experiences of life. It's the loss of wonder, a hitch in our ability to be delighted that for most of us came much easier in childhood.

When I was a kid and read, for example, *The Chronicles of Narnia*, I would see every closet or puddle or painting around me as a potential doorway to another world. I would walk into even familiar closets that had always only held coats and luggage and piles of shoes, close my eyes, and stretch out my hands. I'd wait to feel the ground beneath my feet change from hardwood to pine needles. To hear the crunch of Narnian snow.

Somewhere around adolescence, we're like Adam and Eve in the Garden of Eden, eating from the Tree of Knowledge. We start to see things as they are. Portals close, animals stop talking; we see the sleight of hand behind the magic tricks. We grow self-conscious. It's a normal part of moving from childhood to adulthood, a normal part of growing up.

However, to write and to be engaged with writing, we need to preserve some of the enchantment of childhood. This most clearly applies to those of us who write fiction, but I think it's relevant to writers of nonfiction, too. Whether we're writing a young adult fantasy novel or a piece of creative nonfiction for adults, we have to have some sense that there's more to the world than meets the eye. We're digging through that closet, looking for a point of entry to something deeper, richer, or more expansive that what can be initially comprehended.

Doing that requires a habit of being able to simultaneously hold the knowledge gained when we leave childhood behind *and* the ability to still be enchanted and amazed and curious, to have the eyes to see what others might be missing. If we believe that part of the artist's job in the world is to interpret individual and collective experiences, and make meaning, we need to be able to see past the surface level cycle of action and reaction that feeds algorithms and politics and marketing, adding to an environment that makes cynicism and disillusionment feel like the only rational options. We need our imaginations intact.

What's the cure for disenchantment?

It's not an exaggeration to say that this question is *the* motivating force behind this book, my podcast, all my writing *about* writing and being a writer, and in many ways the content of my novels. My deep faith is that the writing life—the creative life, the life of the mind—holds the answer. My quest to stay engaged and enchanted with the world is part and parcel not only of why I write, but why I choose to think about the writing life in the terms that I do.

Ultimately I do not choose to think of writing as ditch-digging or just another job. I choose to see it as a cure for disenchantment, a stay against cynicism. I choose to believe there's more than meets the eye. I stay open to the possibility that there may be portals to something deeper all around us, and they don't require magic to enter, only attention and curiosity. That's as close as I come to having a spiritual practice these days, and I guess it's also a mini-manifesto.

Disenchantment is always nearby, ready to knock down my lofty talk and provide evidence that my cynicism is earned. I let it in for an occasional visit; I'm only human on a troubled planet. But I can't invite it to move in, or my desire to write and my ability to care will wither and die.

Mistaking "being a writer" for being a writer.

Let's make up an imaginary writer so I don't have to use "you" or "I" here and make us all feel bad. I'm not even going to use a binary gender designation. Let's call them Gen.

Gen has sixteen different programs on their computer that allegedly help them write. Gen is a chronic conference-goer. Gen has been workshopping the same first two chapters of an unfinished novel for twelve years. Gen has an impressive file of inspirational quotes, and reads the blogs and tweets and newsletters of every writer you've ever heard of and a lot you haven't. Gen can outline Robert McKee's *Story* from memory. Gen can answer every question about agents and editors and the publishing business. Gen has a whole shelf of books about writing.

But Gen's writing doesn't seem to improve or go anywhere. Because they aren't doing it.

For whatever reason, they aren't putting the time into their own work. They aren't writing, writing, and writing some more. Gen has forgotten that you don't improve your mile splits by reading about how to improve your mile splits. You don't build calluses on your fingers by watching other people play guitar. Can you get information and inspiration and helpful knowledge? Yes, absolutely. But nothing happens until the knowledge is put into practice. It's like going to Las Vegas and visiting the Paris and the Venetian, taking gondola rides and trips up the Eiffel Tower replica and into the mini-Louvre. You could snap a photo and fool an inattentive Instagram user, but you haven't been to Europe.

The accessories and costumes and vocabulary of "being a writer" are fun and even invigorating. Gen knows this. It all keeps Gen "feeling inspired" and helps them put on that writer identity and find a kind of belonging.

There's nothing wrong with that. As a process junkie myself, I relate to Gen. I think I've read every book there is that details other writers' process in any way, and it's still not enough for me. My appetite for hearing other writers talk about writing is bottomless—I started a whole podcast in part as an excuse to do just that.

But if Gen wants to get past those first two chapters of a novel and get their story into words, onto screen or paper, if Gen wants to try publishing, if Gen wants to grow, Gen has to acknowledge that all the writer accoutrements are not a substitute for writing.

Maybe Gen is scared. Maybe Gen doesn't feel ready. Maybe Gen hasn't dealt with the inevitable discomfort of writing. The only way Gen is going to get over that obstacle is to do some self-examination and determine if they're content with the Vegas version of Europe (maybe they are) or if they want to work up the courage to make the real trip.

Being in the wrong company.

In the previous chapter, I wrote about how a sustainable writing life invites company.

Sometimes we try in good faith to make that happen, yet wind up in the wrong company.

That could mean: a critique group that's flakey or doesn't know how to give helpful feedback, an author you follow that only posts complaints and stirs up drama, a writing buddy who enables your worst habits, an agent that's not right for you, or even a romantic partner who feels threatened by your creative efforts or otherwise doesn't support them.

Choose your people carefully.

If you realize somewhere along the way that the choices you made when you were a previous version of you aren't helpful anymore, you can make some different choices. Of course, not every person in your circle has to come through on every front. You'll have friends that are good for shop talk, friends that know how to be a good writing date, and friends who excel at giving encouragement when you're down.

And we have concentric circles of folks that make up our greater writing community. The people on the outer rings who don't have as much direct impact on your life may be plentiful, but you're not going to ask the same things of them that you'd ask of your closest people.

You can generally afford to be less protective at those outer rings, though depending on your personality and psychology, you might have to be at least a little mindful even at that level.

For example: I joined Twitter in 2008—more or less when it launched into cultural awareness. Over all those years, I followed a lot of people. A *lot*. My feed was full of everyone in my particular field of writing and publishing, plus a bunch of other public figures and a random smattering of people who probably once tweeted something I thought was funny or interesting. All told, I was following close to two-thousand people.

That's too many. I tried using Twitter's lists functions and mute functions and keyword sorting and anything else I could think of to manage all of the *stuff* that was coming at me every time I went onto the site. But I still felt bombarded by the anger, anxiety, questionable humor, drama, and trauma of way too many people. So around 2015, right before I embarked on a long vacation, I ran a plug-in that mass unfollowed everyone. I wanted to scorch the earth, go on vacation, and then come back and rebuild who I followed a little more thoughtfully with my own mental health in mind.

Taking those measures cut down on a variety of unwelcome emotional distractions that were taking something away from my experience of being a writer rather than adding to it.

Of course, it's easier to unfollow people online than to leave a partner who doesn't want you to grow or end a friendship that's feels unhealthy. Those are bigger and more consequential decisions than I can advise on here. All I can say is keep an eye on the effect that the people in your life are having on you and your pursuit of a fulfilling creative life. If necessary, do some work on boundaries and self-love and see where—and to whom—it all leads you.

Self-obsession.

Self-love and care are one thing; self-obsession is something else, and it's a vice that writers can easily fall into. It's where "the life of the mind" becomes "the life of *my* mind, all the time." Where we start saying no to anything that would ask us to get outside our writing bubble and justify it by saying we have a deadline, or we're prioritizing our creativity, or other rationales that sound good. Where our buffer zone becomes less a protection of our writing time and space and more of an impermeable fortress.

As a full-time writer without kids, this is something I have to watch. The nature of my job is to spend lots of time alone and in charge of my own schedule. I mostly live in my head—not only in the writing itself but in the maintaining social media platforms and monitoring book stats. I can calcify in my World of Sara, and if someone wants one or two hours on *their* schedule, I'm reluctant to commit.

This isn't good for my creativity or my imagination. (Or my relationships.) My perspective narrows. At its worst, it leads to depression. As I write this, I'm winding down a special series on the This Creative Life podcast about launching books. On a recent episode, my co-host and I—who were both about to have books out—talked about feeling bad, feeling down, feeling despondent. In our conversation, it occurred to us that maybe humans aren't meant to think about our*selves* so darn much. Book launching season is inherently self-focused, and it was slowly but surely degrading our moods and desire to create.

It comes back to the issue of engagement. To maintain a rich and sustainable creative life, we need to stay engaged not only with our own interiority and imagination, but with the world and life outside our screens and projects. If we stay isolated and overprotect our bubbles, eventually we won't have anything to write about.

Lack of faith.

I proposed in the last chapter that a sustainable writing life is faith-based. If that's true, then there are also opportunities for losing faith over time. Plenty of them.

You're distracted by the news of the world, a lot of which is, let's face it, *not good*.

You feel inadequate to the creative task at hand.

You have no idea what step to take next with your writing project, and you start to worry that you never will.

You begin to believe in your rejections and obstacles more than you believe in your capacity to learn and grow.

You forget why what you're doing matters, and why you ever cared in the first place.

You've fallen behind in your goals and reaching them feels impossible, so why bother?

You regularly have intrusive thoughts like: *No one wants to read this stuff. Why can't it be easier? Why can't there be fewer unknowns? Why did I ever think I could do this? Everything and everyone is working against me.* You might spiral into hopelessness.

If publishing is part of your goal, you find yourself seeking out proof that your ideas will never sell, and agents don't want what you do, and there's no place in publishing for you and your vision. You get caught in envy and bitterness and zero-sum thinking. It gets harder and harder to sit down and do the writing that you want to do.

Does any of this sound familiar?

It does to me. And it's perfectly understandable.

At heart, I'm a pragmatist. I'm not big on "the power of positive thinking," and I don't believe we can manifest success or failure through our thoughts. But I do believe that we can have *some* choices about how we experience life. Some people have more choices and options than others, based on class, race, family of origin, adverse experiences, and economics. Those things are factors no matter how many mantras for success you chant.

I like to live in reality and know what I'm up against, both internally and externally. So I'm not suggesting that these "lack of faith" issues are easily corrected or that they should just be covered over with a smile and some elbow grease.

When I'm feeling and thinking the "lack of faith" stuff, I try to acknowledge those thoughts and maybe talk about them with a writer pal if I'm in the mood. I try to see if there's any truth beneath my fears or complaints. Often, there is. The world *is* always in a crisis. Writing *is* hard. Sometimes I *am* inadequate to the task at hand. The publishing business *is* rife with entrenched problems and frustrations. And yes, it is true that not everyone who wants to be a published writer will get to be one, and not every published writer will get to *keep* being one, and not every project even by an experienced career writer will succeed. This is all just plain reality, and it's not dangerous to acknowledge it.

After acknowledgment, my next step is to remind myself that I don't *have* to do this. I always give myself the option to quit. Or to take a hiatus. Or at least to consider other possibilities for my life outside of writing.

So far, this process has always brought me back to finding my faith again. Sometimes this happens quickly; sometimes I need a good wallow or a long break and a foray into other possible life paths. There may come a day when that doesn't happen, when I decide that the struggle of trying to be a professional writer isn't worth it and I transition to only writing for myself. Or there may even come a day when I stop writing entirely.

For me, it's important to actively choose the writing life, over and over, and sometimes a temporary loss of faith is a necessary catalyst for reminding myself that it is a choice. I also I try to give myself a break about having all of these intrusive thoughts, because they're often

connected to the mother of all obstacles to a fulfilling and sustainable creative life:

Capitalism.

It's known by a lot of names and wears many hats.

Hustle culture, grind culture, monetization, commodification, being in the marketplace of buying and selling writing, aka "the publishing industry."

It's productivity over people, maybe. Assigning value to what we do based on how it might materially profit us or others. Measuring our worth by our sales and income.

A necessary evil. A complicated good. A system that needs to be burned down. A neutral reality.

However you think of it, we have to learn to live alongside and within this system until something better replaces it, and that's what the next section of the book is all about.

ii. life at the corner of art & commerce

12 /
money: my story and a little advice

As I MENTIONED, I've read a *lot* of books about writing. Most of the popular ones, and a good number of lesser-known titles, too. The authors will tell you about their childhoods, their addictions, their marriages. Their trauma, their affairs. Their craft advice and process and unique perspective on the work of being a writer. But one thing that few talk about with any candor is money.

They'll tell you not to write for money, not to plan on making money, and to have a fallback plan for financial stability. In some cases, their material success is obvious and seems to contradict their advice. In others, you get the clear sense that other things pay their bills—often jobs in academia. Others state outright that they never expected to make any money at all on their writing and imply they still feel that way. They would write no matter what.

I'm not looking for numbers. I'm not looking for a royalty report.

What I'm looking for is any admission that one reason writers get into writing, seek publication, and stay in it is to make money. I want to know where the writer came from, economically, and how that factored into their motivation to finish and sell books.

The only book I can think of that addresses this directly is Stephen King's *On Writing*. Most of the others transmit, to me, a vague picture of middle or upper-class upbringing, good colleges, and a clear path to a life in academia with writing as a personal and artistic under-pinning, and a financial add-on at most.

I get the impression that we're not supposed to admit to trying and hoping to earn money, maybe a lot of it. It makes sense. For the type or writer I describe above—someone who already has a good university job and some family money—it would be gauche to openly admit to wanting fat royalty checks, too.

Writers like me, from insecure backgrounds and no clear path to anything, have internalized this. We're all supposed to pretend money is not on our minds. Writers who write for money are sell-outs; writers who don't think about that stuff are artists. It's an unhelpful binary inherited from a literary history dominated by white men from the upper classes, or from an era of patronage when some benefactor was paying a writer's way to make art and they didn't need to rely on an audience, per se.

Meanwhile, in reality, most of us struggle under the burden of capitalism and have regular anxiety about making ends meet. We might be stuck in jobs we hate, and we have some writing skill and some knowledge about the business, and we see a possible window of escape from the problem of having work that neither creates economic stability *nor* leaves us with any time to practice writing.

But from the moment I put fingers to keys to write my first novel, my intent was to get paid, to attempt to pry that window open for myself. I grew up in enough financial instability that I've always struggled with a deep-seated scarcity mindset and other cognitive habits and patterns that can be summed up by the phrase "poor kid thinking." Some of you know exactly what I mean. It looks like an obsessive focus on what I don't have or what I could lose; a pervading fear that I don't have enough (time, money, groceries, clothes, etc.). If at any point I do have enough, I worry that soon or at some point in the future I won't, so I need to stay worried. And it's not based on nothing. My parents were broke, struggled throughout my childhood, and I grew up in a context of hand-me-downs, handouts, food stamps, and "we can't afford that" worries. There's no family money coming my way. I married into a more stable situation, but not so stable that I never have to worry.

Because of all of this, I harbored from very early on fantasies of some big payday that would mean I'd never have to worry again. My relationship with money could fill its own book (and maybe one day I'll write that), but it's enough for our purposes to say yes, my desire to be a writer has always been tied into my need to make money and my drive to create some economic stability for myself.

It's ironic because one of the first things working writers will tell you (myself included) is that writing is *not* a path to financial stability. But for reasons that have to do with my background, my personality, my damage, and my skill set, I always felt that writing was as good a path as any to that for me, and it was the only one I could see with any clarity. I had no career ambitions outside of it, no sense of what else I might be good at.

This need coupled with the longing to tell the stories I had up in my head propelled me through that decade of learning how to write and revise and educating myself about the publishing business. It kept me going through a series of jobs I didn't want. It gave me something to daydream about. It gave me an identity and a motivation.

The day I got my first book offer, I was working part-time at a job that paid eleven dollars an hour. It didn't take a huge offer to top my annual salary, and I soon quit to become a "full-time writer." That was 2005, and I've been living with that decision for better and worse ever since.

I guess it would be nice and perhaps more palatable to others to be able to say I was driven purely by passion, the love of the story, the engagement with the process, and the satisfaction of seeing something finished. All those things *were* in play, but it was the thought of money, of making it a career, that pushed me to the finish line that was also the starting line of my career.

I don't judge myself or anyone else for whom money is a motivation. I mean, I don't *want* money to intrude on my creative process; I do try to keep a separation. But we live in a world where we need money to survive. We have to have money to exchange for food, clothing, and shelter, and whether it's writing or something else, most of us have to get that money through some kind of work. Unless you're willing to make some very radical life choices, there's not really any opting out of that system.

So I come to this topic of art and commerce from that reality; I don't know of another one.

I've heard a lot of working writers say something along the lines of: if you *can* do anything else for money, you should. I've thought it myself and half believe it. Maybe if I had a time machine and could find some kind of work I didn't hate while I was still active in the job market, I would, and take that pressure off my writing. I don't know. By now, the two things—writing and making a living (using a very loose definition of "a living")—are entwined for me at the root.

Now for the advice.

If you're still in a place where you're able to provide financial stability for yourself by doing something else, and you don't hate it, I encourage you to see that as a gift to your writing life. Take the regular paychecks (and, hopefully, health insurance) and use them in service of cultivating a writing life. Take classes, use PTO to give yourself writing days, get yourself the six-dollar coffee as a reward for getting your words in. If you have more disposable income, buy all the gadgets and writing books, go on retreats and to conferences, maybe even build a writing shed in the yard. Do you have much more than enough? Contribute to the broader writing community and culture. Sponsor young writers so they can go to conferences and take classes, donate to organizations that help lift up diverse voices, buy stacks of books from your local bookshop. And keep writing and seeing the world through the lenses of curiosity and attention, keep living the life of the mind.

Maybe having more than enough doesn't describe you, and you know you're the kind of person who can't thrive in uncertain conditions. You feel a lot of stress when your bank balance is low, and you're up at night calculating how many months of living expenses you'd have if you lost your job tomorrow. Writing may not be the career choice for you. Which doesn't mean you can't write and be published, just that for the sake of your sanity, you won't rely on it to feed and shelter and clothe you.

If you hate your job or it's so draining that working up the energy to write and do the creating that you want to do feels impossible, especially if that's combined with parenting and/or taking care of older family members, you're not alone. Maybe you can find a way to cobble together a few different gigs to relieve some of that "I hate my job" stress, or find a less-bad situation. But try not to see a day job as the enemy of writing, and try not to see writing as the answer to your financial problems.

Of course, that advice makes me a hypocrite.

So if you're like me and you've already gone all-in on writing, or you're about to, or you want to and you won't really be satisfied until you can, well, hello, I see you.

Whichever category we're in, we all have to at least think about how we want to negotiate life at the intersection of art and commerce. Avoiding it entirely is a valid choice, if you make it with intention. But most of us—especially if we want to share what we write—are going to come in at least occasional contact with the traffic.

13 /
to market, to market

THE PUBLISHING MARKETPLACE is an arena of commerce and competition. There are producers and sellers of books (or articles, short stories, poems, screenplays, "content") and buyers, also known as an audience —though not all audience are buyers and not all buyers are audience. There are systems and machines built to provide structure for buyers and sellers and products, i.e. what makers make. In that system, writers generally write *for* someone.

The question of *who* we write for is more complex than it may seem on its face.

I put myself in the category of writers who start out writing for themselves. I'm following something that's captivated *my* imagination. I'm trying to translate it into language, into a story, as a way to understand why it grabbed me in the first place, or to answer a question I need to write through in order to clarify it. That's how it starts for me.

But I just said in the last chapter that I've always written with the intent to get paid!

It isn't an either/or paradigm. I can follow a creative spark for myself, and then in the act of translating something that feels unformed and abstract into language for my own satisfaction and comprehension, it becomes potentially consumable by anyone else who can read. In the act of writing, I *am* trying to put it into a familiar shape—in my case, a novel, by the western, modern definition of "novel" that I grew up with. So at the end of the endeavor I started for myself, I have a thing that, when revised and edited and proofread and bound or collected into an electronic file, can be a product in a category that most people are generally familiar with, and I did it on purpose.

However, in the act of writing—especially in the early stages of the process—I'm rarely thinking about the end user or the marketplace. There are other writers who have an audience in mind from the beginning.

For a while, I had an all-access subscription to the MasterClass site. If you're not familiar with it, it features extended video classes led by known experts in various fields. For example, Gordon Ramsay teaching you how to cook, or Serena Williams teaching tennis technique, or St. Vincent teaching songwriting. There are lots of classes in the writing category taught by people like Shonda Rhimes, David Sedaris, and Margaret Atwood. And there's one taught by James Patterson.

Patterson is a *little* bit my nemesis, though he doesn't know it, and if he did, would not care. It's nothing personal. I of course had to hate-watch some of his class. As a writer of what we call commercial fiction (a general category term encompassing a range of genres that sell to the widest reading public), Patterson comes from a specific point of view, and a lot of his advice is geared toward how to write books that will sell. At one point, he actually says something like, "Don't write a good thriller; write a popular thriller." As if these things are mutually exclusive. Don't write good books, says he, write books that sell.

Now, that's not *my* thing, but the man does know whereof he speaks when it comes to selling. He's among the top five richest writers in the world. Whether you hate that fact or admire it, I know he's not worrying about paying for his health insurance, and he makes a case for writing with an audience—a *market*—in mind.

That's one approach. Mine is another. And there are others. No matter how you frame it for yourself, it behooves anyone trying to get paid to at know even in a general way what's happening in the market they are trying to get into.

We can acknowledge right here and now that we cannot control the marketplace. We can't know what's going to be popular next year, or predict world events that will impact what people want to read. At the same time, we can recognize that doesn't mean keeping ourselves ignorant about how the publishing business works—in general and in the various niches relevant to us.

My approach to the business side of writing can be summed up by a fun Jesus quote that doesn't get the cross-stitch treatment it deserves: "Be as shrewd as snakes and as innocent as doves."

What do I mean by that? I try to know as much as I possibly can about the publishing industry, including who's who, what's selling, what an editor's recent acquisitions tell me about what they're looking for, how much does this website pay for long-form essays, how much did that writer get from that journal for a short story, what kinds of advances are my peers getting, what types of novels seem to be falling out of favor, which of my books do readers respond to most, why did this publicist move to a different publishing house, why did that editor leave the business, where is my contract and what does it say, what kinds of questions do I need to ask my agent next time we talk to understand the current publishing landscape, et cetera. That's the "shrewd as snakes" part. I like to live in reality and have my eyes open.

But when it comes to the *act of writing*, I have to shut the door on all that strategic knowledge and become an innocent. If I talk myself out of a story idea I love because I'm worried the market won't want it and instead try to direct myself—a la Patterson's advice—to write "a poplar book," or something I don't care about but think the market will reward me for, I'm in trouble.

Do I use my knowledge and experience to try to be strategic about deciding what to write? Yes. But it's not my north star. I have to protect the deepest place where the good work lives from all that savvy. For one thing, that's no guarantee that the "write a popular book" mindset is going to actually result in me writing a popular book. For another thing, "make it popular" quickly becomes an intrusive voice that stifles my creativity and scrambles my writing instincts.

Again, that's me. Each writer has to forge her own relationship with the marketplace and an audience, and determine how big a role that plays in the creative process. I've got friends who approach work with much more audience-strategy than I do and that pays off for them, and friends who do well by rarely thinking about audience.

In any case, working writers are always making creative decisions within the context of the market, to a greater or lesser extent. I'm not suggesting one approach is superior. What I am suggesting is that if you want to write for publication, you can't steer completely clear of the business side of it. Figuring out your own tolerance for it will be a matter of learning as you go. If you're just starting out, learn what you can about the industry, but don't spend more time on that than you do on your writing. Understand genres and categories and their respective audiences, but don't let it pull you off the course your creative compass wants to set. Try to keep up with what's going on "out there," but don't get obsessed with it "in here," that is, the place you write from.

Work out a balance of art and commerce that allows you to stay in touch with your writing voice while also having an idea of where it might fit into the marketplace. Recalibrate as needed.

14 /
the middle of the beginning

WHEN I FIRST MET THE person who would become my present-day literary agent, I was over seven years into my sincere attempt at being a novelist. I'd already had and lost one agent. I'd written three complete novels. One went as far as a publisher's acquisitions meeting before it was rejected; one won a state arts council prize for an unpublished novel. But after all that time, there I was again with no agent, nothing on submission to publishers, feeling like I was back to square one and trying to find representation for my fourth attempt at a novel.

I sat across from this man I desperately wanted to represent me, and I told him my story and all the things that had and hadn't happened so far, and I started to get emotional. I had to stop talking so I wouldn't ugly-cry in front of a stranger.

In the uncomfortable silence, he said something like, "It's really hard when you're not a beginner anymore but you haven't broken through yet."

All I could do at the time was nod and take a tissue from the box on his desk and attempt to blow my nose in a non-disgusting manner. But I wanted to say, "Yes it *is*, that's it exactly," and I've since repeated his words to many writers who are where I was back then.

There's a decent chance that if you're reading this book, this describes you. Not a total beginner. Maybe you've been in writing groups and gone to some conferences. Maybe you've gotten an MFA. Maybe you've been on the receiving end of encouraging feedback and near-successes. Placed an essay or story here or there, gotten a poem published, written a popular blog post. Maybe you've even had a book published that slipped quietly into the night. You could be in the middle of your beginning, or the beginning of your middle. But you wonder if it's the end.

This stage is difficult! Not only that, I think it's the time we're most in danger of losing our creative faith and fire.

This is when the intrusive voices from within or without swoop in. Maybe it's a family member saying, "You've given this a shot, and it didn't work out. Time to move on." Maybe it's a coworker who asks an innocent question like, "Are you still writing?" and all you can hear is, "You're *still* trying that writing thing?" Or, more than likely, the voice is coming from inside the house, and you're the one saying these things to yourself. And wondering if there's a point in continuing to try.

I want to be very clear about something: It is okay to

stop. It's okay to not be a published writer! It's okay to quit writing entirely and do something else that makes that part of you happy. As I've written elsewhere in this book, I've "quit" many times, myself, and have to periodically check in to make sure it's something I'm actively choosing. It's *okay* to not choose writing, or to let go of a dream that feels like it's turning on you.

The danger I'm talking about pertains to those of you who know you don't want to quit trying to get your work published or get it published better, who strive to level up, but who also feel like you're spinning your wheels. You get rejections and react to the feedback and change your project, then send it out again only to get feedback that contradicts the earlier feedback. Your writing has been workshopped so much that you start to wonder if it's getting *worse*. You sign with an agent and then they ghost you. You get an opportunity then find out it's a scam. An editor acquires your work and then quits, leaving your project orphaned. You get published, but it flops. You get published, but it hurts.

Most of these things happened to me somewhere along the way, and it feels awful, and it's hard to keep going. But this is the time when, if you *know* you want this, you've got to hang on. Those near-success experiences mean something. The almost-wins aren't nothing. The editor or agent who saw something in your work before they disappeared were on to something.

Picture it like being in a long line for a Disney ride. It can feel eternal. You're hot and hungry and you have to pee and you can't imagine at this point that it's even going to be worth it. You're not at the end of the line anymore, but you're not convinced it's moving. Sometimes you see someone seem to jump the line, or get waved in by a friend, or they bought their way into the Lightning Lane. It hardly seems fair. But if you want to take that ride, all you have to do is stay in line.

This is where the metaphor breaks down a little because there's no guarantee in publishing that you'll eventually get to take the ride. But there *is* a guarantee that if you get out of line, you won't.

Sometimes we need to take breaks from submitting and querying. Sometimes we need to let go of a project and start something new. Sometimes we need to get offline—especially those times when it seems like everyone you know and their cousin are getting book deals. Sometimes we need to give ourselves a break from writing and get into some other creative thing like crafts or painting or music or cooking while we wait for the business side of writing to better align with what we're doing. We need to refill our creative well, tend to the spark. But then we need to get back to work.

I want to be careful to not make false promises. That's a pitfall of the grifters I refer to at the beginning of this book, and a pitfall of the Girlboss-Try-Harderism of success culture. But the tenacity I'm talking about is not the same thing as blind optimism. And unlike in an MLM scheme, you do not need to spend your life savings in the pursuit of writing for publication, or drag your friends and family into a scam. I'm just saying a version of what I said in the "Talent" chapter: what's more important than innate giftedness is perseverance and persistence. At craft, at deepening your inner life to make the work better, and yes, at the business side of the whole endeavor. If you want to take this ride, stay in line until they close it down.

15 /
platforms & choices

IF YOU'VE GOT any relationship whatsoever with the writing business, or have done even the littlest bit of research, you've probably heard something like "you need a platform." You may have been told that you "have to" be on social media.

The only "have to" when it comes to being a writer is writing. Everything after that—to share or not to share, to try to get published, to have a platform, to have a website, to be on social media, to make swag, to hold giveaways, to have an opinion on every publishing controversy that comes along, and whatever else you've been told is a must —is a choice.

Naturally, different choices have different potential consequences.

If you decide not to have an online presence, that might make it harder to get the word out about your writing or connect with others. Or it might make you intriguing and mysterious.

Being "very online" and making all the connections and sharing about who you are and what you think could help you when it's time to sell a book or article. Or it could put people off if they don't like what you have to say.

Publishing your work (traditionally or independently) might make you some money and bring you the satisfaction of closing that circle of writer and reader. Or it might stress you out and make you miss the love of writing you had before anyone knew about it.

My point here is to make choices that you think are going to work for *you*—your schedule, your personality, your skillset, your interests. Don't do things just because someone said you should. Or go ahead and try it, see what you think, and adjust accordingly. It's all up to you. I know writers who have kind of gone off the social grid after being very online, and I know writers who were never on the grid, and writers who are very happy with staying active on all possible grids.

My advice has always been to do what's fun or easy for you, and don't force anything else. And if being online starts to encroach on your mental health, your work habits, your connection to yourself and your writing, then take a break. There's no one right way to do it, and it's never more important than the actual writing you produce.

16 /
going to new york

YEARS AGO, I heard a writer speak at a local book festival. Someone in the audience asked him his advice for writers who want to publish, and he said something like, "Go to the center ring of the circus. Go to New York." He went on to explain that he meant go for success in traditional publishing, particularly for what we then called the "big six" publishers, now the "big five," and maybe soon the "big four." New York City is the capitol of that world, or at least the geographical metaphor for it.

What I took from that was that anyone who wants to publish should go right for the big prize—a contract with a publishing institution—rather than starting out smaller, local, or on the fringes. And why not? There's nothing at stake when you're brand new; no need to be shy and limit yourself from the jump by only thinking of small presses, university presses, or self-publishing.

I think the "why not" for a lot of people is a mistaken

belief that there's no chance of breaking into NYC publishing unless you already know someone. I've heard this stated outright by writers on panels at conferences. "It's all who you know," they say. "You have a better chance of winning the lottery than of getting published by one of the big houses." It drives me nuts to hear this because there are countless stories, including my own, to disprove it. Writers can and do break into Big Publishing all the time without having a referral or connection. In fact, it's probably the norm.

It's true that you can be stuck in the submit-revise-rejection-submit-revise-rejection phase for what feels like a cruel eternity. Wait times through the big houses and experienced agents are long. Getting attention is difficult. And the longer writers are in that phase, the more connections they make along the way, and eventually it may look to the outside that they benefited from a "who you know" situation when in reality they started cold.

Yes, knowing people is a good thing and can help you get opportunities you might not otherwise have. But those "people you know" have to genuinely connect with your work, see evidence of your experience and capability, or have some other good reason to believe you can do what you say you can. Even a rave referral from an experienced writer who loves what you're doing doesn't mean their agent will sign you on the spot. They have to believe they can sell your work.

I think the "it's who you know" folks say this because

they're looking for a way to explain to themselves why things haven't yet happened for their writing the way they'd planned. They don't want it to be about yet another revision, moving on to a new idea, taking a class, or persisting through the boring and eternal waits that are part of the traditional publishing process. It's true that publishing is very competitive and there are only so many slots per season in a publisher's catalog, and you generally need an agent even to be read. You do have to work for it, and you do need a lot of patience. But you don't have to know someone.

It may be that what you write is perfectly suited to medium or small presses, or religious publishers or other niche operations. In that case, it makes sense to start there and see where it takes you.

But if what you write is fairly mainstream and you dream of being in traditional Big Publishing but don't know anyone else who writes and you live in the middle of a cornfield and think you're not allowed to play in the center ring, this is your permission to go for it. Send your stuff to your dream agent, to top-tier journals, to well-paying sites. See if you can get yourself a big fat book deal from an international conglomerate.

If in time you sense no movement on that front, you can start working your way through the next batch of agents that you've researched, the medium-sized publishers and small presses, editors that will read unagented manuscripts, university presses—wherever seems like it might be a good fit for what you're doing.

But don't disqualify yourself from what you want before you even try.

As I wrote at the start of this section, part of *going for it* is acquiring as much knowledge as you can about how traditional publishing works. What is the acquisitions process? What's the editorial process? How are books marketed? How are they edited? How do cover design and titling work? How do you work with an agent for a successful collaboration? How do you work with an editor as a first-time writer and not feel intimidated by them or feel like you're going to lose your voice?

If you don't have a mentor or mentors on tap to help you work through these questions, there are other ways to learn. When I first started, *way* before I was even ready to tell anyone that I wanted to write, I gobbled up interviews with writers and editors and publishing professionals, I read biographies, watched documentaries, listened to writers talk at my local book festival—which was free to attend. Then I started paying to go to conferences, bought a subscription to *Poets & Writers,* enrolled in workshops. Shortly before I signed with my second and present agent, I was starting to look into MFA programs.

When I started, it was ancient Internet times, but there were still ways to eavesdrop on writers talking amongst themselves in chat rooms. Now you can watch authors talk on social media. You can follow agents and editors. You can listen to podcasts, watch YouTube, scour message boards.

Try to give yourself a well-rounded education about

how it all works, as your resources and time allow. I'm an information hound (a Type Five by the Enneagram; if you know you know). When I was a kid, I pored over encyclopedias and dictionaries. As an adult, Wikipedia and Google are two of my best friends. So the self-education part of becoming a writer came naturally to me and I enjoyed it. I know not everyone is like that. Some writers have to push themselves to dive in to the business research, and get quickly overwhelmed and confused. Neuro-divergence may be in play; different learning styles need different approaches. Try to figure out what works for you. Maybe short-form video is how you learn best. Or maybe you want to do the ten-hour MasterClass for your niche, or invest in another online course that can teach you the basics.

If you have the resources to get an MFA, that may be your path. But most programs won't tell you much about how the business works. Some writers from that academic background even have the mindset that they don't want to "dirty themselves" with all that businessy stuff. If that's you, I'd direct you back to the "To Market, To Market" chapter, to read my philosophy about getting industry savvy while keeping your creative process as unsullied as possible.

A *few* people are so magnificently and uniquely talented that they write something brilliant, stumble into publishing, never need to know how it works, and use their royalties to buy a hundred acres in the woods and only their agent and mom know how to reach them. Is this you? Burn this book. Everyone else, consider making it part of your process to learn how the business works, how the money works, and how to navigate the system as the one with the intellectual property on offer. Take it to the biggest market there is and see what happens.

17 /
going indie

WHAT IF YOU want to share your work through the act of publishing and selling (hopefully) to readers, but the traditional publishing world doesn't want to let you in? What if you don't *want* them to want you? What if you try them and don't like what you experience? What if you try them, and it's fine, great, super, but sometimes you also want to do your own thing?

The answer to all of these questions is: self-publishing. (To clarify terms: I'm using "self-publishing" and "indie-publishing" interchangeably in this book, though indie-publishing is a category that many people use to mean or include small, medium, and hybrid independent presses).

Self-publishing is not the answer I would not have given twenty or even ten years ago.

When I started my serious pursuit of writing for publication, it was the 1990s and self-publishing as we know it today didn't exist. Self-publishing was often known then as "vanity publishing," and if you can't guess from that terminology, it held a certain stigma. It was publishing for people who, more than anything, wanted their name on a book. They may or may not have tried traditional routes. For some, it was a last resort. For others, it was the first tack.

Vanity publishing worked something like this: you wrote your book, perhaps paid to have it edited, and then paid a company to typeset and print your book. You then paid for finished copies of the book. A lot of finished copies. Before the print-on-demand technology we have today that allows print runs of even a single book, you were working with the printer's minimum print runs. You could wind up with cases and cases of copies of your book. Then it was up to you to do what you wanted with them. You could try walking into bookstores in hopes of convincing them to stock it, or you could sell it to your friends, or give it away. There was really no wholesale distribution available, little to no advertising or marketing, and the ultimate outcome for most writers was being out upwards of ten grand with nothing to show for it but a garage full of books, slowly growing mold.

There were exceptions. Some very niche nonfiction could do alright if the writer was willing to travel around with books in the trunk of their car and sell at conference tables and to specialized bookstores. Intrepid writers with marketing savvy and those who knew how to stake out a claim in the early days of the Internet could do good business. But it was a lot of work and wasn't what most writers were looking for in a publishing experience.

Ergo, any time someone asked me back then if they should pursue self-publishing, the answer was a resounding, "No."

All of that changed with the advent of the Amazon era, e-books, and e-reader technology, and *really* changed when Amazon introduced its KDP (Kindle Direct Publishing) platform in 2007, compelling other companies (Apple, Barnes & Noble, Kobo, etc.) to follow suit. Those things coupled with the rise of social media and access to simple e-commerce options meant that there were suddenly accessible ways for individual writers to publish, market, distribute, and sell their own books at a fraction of the cost of the old vanity press model. Or no cost at all, if a writer is equipped to edit, proofread, and design everything themself.

So does the access to this process mean you should you skip trying to jump through all the traditional publishing hoops and go straight to striking out on your own?

There's no simple answer to that, but I fall somewhere between "not necessarily" and "not yet."

I still think most writers are better off with the structure and support that a traditional publisher provides, if they can break in. The machinery of big publishers may be slow, but it's got a lot of parts that are specifically made for the complementary machinery of distributors, booksellers, and readers. Writers are typically paid some money upfront, in the form of an advance vs. shelling it out of pocket. As part of their investment in a book, publishers provide developmental editing, copyediting, and proofreading; cover design and interior design; catalog placement, marketing, and publicity. If you're in children's publishing, there's a whole department that deals in marketing and selling to schools and libraries. Finally, you get distribution to booksellers—Amazon, Apple, and chain stores along with independent bookstores, both online and off. Also, a traditional publisher might handle subrights such as translation into other languages, or the production of other formats like audio and paperback. Once you're in the machine, it's all set up to handle everything at no cost to you. They make money by selling your books and taking their cut, not by charging you upfront for publication services.

However...

The machine giveth, and the machine taketh away.

Being part of a big machine means you can fall through the cracks. If there's not sustained publisher excitement about your book by the time it comes out, it can be left to sink or swim. Sinking could look like the promised marketing dollars not coming your way, stores not ordering the book if it's not getting a little extra push from sales, you as the author not getting pitched for conferences and panels, the publisher not actively managing the subrights.

Or, the publisher could do everything right, everything they promised, and your book could *still* get lost among a sea of others. When that happens, you're left feeling helpless because unless your agent can work some magic for you, your hands *are* kind of tied. The publisher still holds whatever rights you sold to them in the initial deal (e.g. world English in all formats, North American rights, world rights, etc.) Even if they're not actively doing anything to help push your book, as long as they hold the rights and sell an extremely minimal number of copies every year, you can't do anything with the book— that book you worked very hard on—either.

It's far from a perfect system. It's not for every author or every book at all times.

After over fifteen years and ten books worth of experience in traditional publishing, I've come to believe that every writer, whether already traditionally published and experienced or brand new to the whole thing, can benefit from at least knowing how the self-publishing process works. Writers can be a little ground up in all that machinery, and having the tools to self-publish can help us get back some control, or at least give us options.

This book is my first self-published project. I did not try to sell it to a traditional publisher; I planned from the beginning to do it all myself. It's a small and perhaps niche project—a companion book to a podcast that's by no means a blockbuster. It's not a craft book, but it's also not pure inspiration. I wanted to write something both practical and philosophical for the kind of writer who enjoys listening to other writers talk about various aspects of the writing life. I knew it would be short, and I knew it would be loose. I wanted it to feel conversational, almost like a collection of blog posts but with more of an intentional shape and overall effect.

My vision all felt suited to the self-publishing paradigm. And—back to the money topic—a big part of the appeal was removing the pressure I always feel with an advance. I can tend to be overly concerned with thoughts like, "my publisher has paid me x dollars to write this book; they've invested in it, they own it, and I have to live up to *their* expectations for it." It can be immobilizing on the creative front.

Lastly, after so many books where I was working on the publisher's and editor's schedule, and with all the tentacles of that machine, the idea of getting to run the whole show myself was enticing. From the schedule and the cover to the total power over all the rights, I'm the boss. I know I can publish excerpts of whatever length wherever I want, make my own audio, update and correct any errors myself, experiment with ads, put out future new editions, and set my own prices.

All of this sweet, sweet control comes with some downsides. I'm paying upfront for a professional copyeditor and proofreader. There was no developmental editor to stop me from saying something dumb or help me organize the content. I'm handling the design and layout aspects myself (with the help of some software), and that has involved a learning curve. And if it all flops? I'll have no one to blame but myself.

I enjoy learning, though, and acquiring skills, and I've

gotten a lot out of this process. By doing *this* project, I'm now ready to deploy these skills in the future if there's anything else I write that seems suited to the self-publishing paradigm.

Through it, I've also grown to feel strongly that every established author should seriously consider giving it a go. Those who learn how to use the distribution platforms and the marketing and publicity facets of indie-publishing are at an advantage the next time they have a project outside of their established brand, something they're having trouble placing, or rights to old work revert back to them. Or if they're tired of being at the mercy of the machine, they can try this approach to regain a sense of autonomy and perhaps even an appreciation of what the machine *does* provide.

For an author with an already-established brand, discoverability is not as much of a concern, nor is any remaining stigma around self-publishing. Most readers shopping for books, especially online, won't be able to distinguish between the traditional and self-published titles of a given author.

For debut authors, the situation is a bit different. Discoverability becomes an issue. There are well over a million (it's closer to two) self-published titles pouring into the market every year. If you don't already have some sort of audience through social media and/or newsletters, or through establishment in some other arena (business, influence, entertainment), it can be difficult for your book to find readers and vice versa. Certain niches do better in self-publishing than others—romance, paranormal, new adult, and deeper niches within those genres always have hungry readers. Literary fiction? Not so much. How-to books can do well, and so can other very specific nonfiction. Memoir and personal essays? Maybe not.

Figuring out if your work is poised to do as well or better in indie-publishing as it could in traditional will take some careful research and analysis. Even then, writers without established names have to knock it out of the park in terms of cover design, titles, and having savvy (or the money to pay for someone else's) about all the things that help readers find your books—SEO, keywords, targeted ads, attractive pricing. Not to mention developmental editing with a freelance editor, as well as copyediting and proofreading, to make sure the work itself is solid.

It's possible, though. And for more and more writers, it's a way around the slow machinery of big publishing and the gatekeeping that sometimes comes with it.

I stand by the advice to "go to New York" if you're just starting out and want the best chance at finding readers, but if you hit a dead end on that path, there are alternate routes that might be better for you.

18 /
going pro

Traditionally-published, self-published, or both; full-time or part-time or weekends only; long-form or short-form, fiction or nonfiction; if you are writing regularly with the intent to publish, and engaging with people and systems that will help you do that, you are on the path to becoming a professional writer or you already are one.

We can quibble over terms like "professional writer" and "working writer" and "freelance writer," and what exactly qualifies you to be in those categories. To me it's more of a mindset than anything. You've probably heard the advice to "treat your writing like a business." I'd modify that to—treat your writing like a business *if* you want it to be a business. If you want to be published and sell books, you can't treat it like a hobby you only get around to when you feel like it.

At the same time, treating writing like a business isn't the be-all and end-all of it. It's a means to an end—having your work reach people—not the end itself. We don't want the "professional" crowding out the "writer," i.e. all the loftier stuff about the life of the mind and the habits of attention and curiosity that lead to good work that is going to connect to people and, perchance, sell.

My metaphor for this part of the book has been that art and commerce are an intersection, a crossroads. Crossroads are meant to join two paths and give you the option of going further down one or another, depending on your ultimate destination. You don't park in the middle and stay there. There's a time to mosey further down the art road, away from the traffic, and a time to hustle down the crowded, noisy streets of industry.

Part of being a professional is knowing when to retreat and when to shift into boss mode. When you're starting out, you don't want to get too far down the commerce road until you've gotten sure-footed on the art path. That might mean limiting your industry research time, or unfollowing or unsubscribing from accounts and newsletters that overly focus on the business side. When you're in a vulnerable art-making stage, the last thing you need is a feed and inbox full of announcements of all your peers doing exciting things for boatloads of money.

Then, when you've got a finished thing and you've deployed all your ability in the interest of making it good, you can tuck it under your arm and walk, run, bike, drive, or Lyft back to the crossroads and take a turn onto commerce street. Smile and tip your hat at people. Introduce yourself. Say, "This is what I have. This is what I made. What's happening here, and how does this thing I have to offer fit into it?" You might look around awhile and pop into all the stores and decide you need to head back to art road and do some more work.

Through your writing life and pursuit of a career, you'll return to this crossroads again and again, from one path or the other. The further you go down the commerce side, the more willpower and intent it can take to step back and find a side road that's going to get you back to art—the habits of the mind, the daily practice of creativity, a place of contemplation instead of reaction. This is especially true for writers who are lucky enough to be regularly published. We could have a lot of commerce and industry happening for a finished work, while we're also in the process of generating something new. That means living closer to the crossroads for a time and finding ways to block out the traffic noise.

Okay, so given all that—the need for balance, the understanding that "treat it like a business" is not the endgame—what are some characteristics and habits of a professional writer?

It's not about how many deals you have, writing every day, or getting a certain royalty check.

It *is* about:

Having a regular writing habit or discipline.

This needn't be every day, no matter what other authors may say. If you consistently write for six hours every weekend, ninety minutes every other day, an hour on days that have an "r" in them, a certain number of words a week . . . how*ever* you want to work it, that's a regular discipline. It just means you don't wait until you feel like writing or until everything else is done. You may rarely feel like writing, and there will always be to-do lists.

Developing a sense of what's suited to public communication and what's best kept private. I can't tell you how many times in any given week I see a writer tweet or post something that makes me think, "Do they not have a group text or chat?" Never forget that unless your accounts are private, everyone can see what you say! Also, even in private conversation, screenshots are a thing. A little circumspection is a good thing for a professional to develop.

Making it your business to understand anything you sign. Even if you have an amazing literary agent or lawyer you trust to vet your contracts, you should read them. Ask questions if there's something you don't understand.

Having a grasp of basic business and human etiquette. Yes, publishing can be a very personal and casual industry, but it's still great to thank people, respect boundaries, and avoid spreading gossip. This is your choice of course, and if you would like to establish yourself as a misanthrope, hermit, crank, or the queen of all tea, go right ahead. But never forget the lessons of Bad Art Friend[1].

Understanding a healthy separation between reader and writer. Some writers have built great careers by being *very* engaged with their readers, and that's certainly an option. Think carefully about it, though. That can mean spending a lot more time at a very busy spot in the crossroads, and your inner compass and writing habits can suffer. You can also be tempted to do things like respond to reviews, get involved in little interpersonal dramas among readers, and write "to order" vs. what you want. The happiest writers I know keep a healthy boundary there and take the approach that once a book is out, it belongs to readers. We can let go and move on.

Owning privileges. It's important to continually do the work of understanding various privileges—not only race, but also gender and gender identity, sexuality, body size, ability, class, mental or physical health status, skin color, religion, etc.—and how they work in the world and in publishing, and to take the active steps we can toward making it more equitable for all writers and readers.

Managing money. Especially if you're working in book-length projects (that tend to involve more money), you want to be ready the first time you get paid a chunk of change. Make it part of your business to understand your payout structure, tax obligations, how to budget for work-related expenses (travel, equipment, office space), and whether you should establish a business entity like an LLC or S-Corporation. If all this is as overwhelming to you as it is to me, hire a CPA. It's worth it.

Accepting limitations. We all have limitations, and ideally they'll inform decisions about how to be the public writer version of yourself. You don't have to give up your privacy. You don't have to share everything. You don't have to answer every email seeking free advice. You don't have to do events. You don't have to put your face online. You don't have to like all your author friends' posts or even read all their books. You can choose how much to give outside of the writing itself.

At the beginning of our lives as writers, we pour a lot of energy into, well, learning how to write. That's as it should be, and it's an ongoing endeavor. That's why this Art & Commerce section is sandwiched between two sections on the inner work of the writing life. If part of your goal is sharing and publishing, though, you're going to be out in the marketplace to some degree. Ultimately, there is no one right way to do this. You'll figure it out as you go. It will be part of the overall arc of your life as a writer, which—as we'll talk about in the next section—actually never ends.

---

1. https://www.nytimes.com/2021/10/05/magazine/dorland-v-larson.html

iii. the internal arc

19 /
inside the labyrinth

At the beginning of this book, I compared the writing life to a labyrinth.

Then I found this quote about the type of labyrinth I mean:

> *There is no right or wrong way to walk a labyrinth. . . . You find yourself confused and "lost" on the path. You have an awkward moment as you meet a fellow walker on the same path. You become irritated that there are too many people in the labyrinth. You are determined to find the "answer" but instead experience nothing. . . Walking . . . balancing . . . people . . . perseverance . . . On the path we meet every and all things.*[1]

I can't think of a better way to describe how a writing life feels over the long term.

When I started out, I thought that once I had one book

published—had *one* successful outing as a writer with my name on a book and a few good reviews—the rest would come a lot easier. I would have arrived, and while writing would always be challenging, there'd be certain things I'd never have to deal with again. For instance, the fear of failure, uncertainty and self-doubt, not feeling good enough, wondering if I had a place in the world of writers and writing. All of that would be solved. I'd be on a ladder, stepping onto higher rungs every year and with every book.

In reality, the further into the labyrinth of the writing life I've gone, the more I've encountered confusion and uncertainty. I've felt more lost in the last ten years of doing this than in the first ten. Imposter syndrome makes a visit regularly, especially when I'm tired. I've had setbacks that couldn't be helped. I've been sidetracked by personal crises and thwarted by my own decisions. I've been paid well at times and still worry about money all the time. Wherever I thought I was about to find an answer, I encountered more questions. Every book I write presents a new challenge; I rarely feel like I know what I'm doing.

And yes, there are awkward moments with "fellow walkers" and sometimes way too many people.

But overall? Thank God for other writers, especially the ones who are willing to be honest. Through those friendships and conversations, I know I'm not alone in these experiences. Starting my podcast and writing this book are my ways of trying to keep reminding myself that this *is* a labyrinth, not a ladder, and to offer that perspective to anyone who needs it.

This next section is about digging a little deeper into the long view. The "walking . . . balancing . . . people . . . perseverance" of it all. What it means to meet every and all things.

———————————————

1. http://www.wtc.perth.anglican.org/wp-content/uploads/2016/06/Guidelines-for-Walking-the-Labyrinth.pdf

20 /
writing won't fix your childhood (but it might help)

I WAS BORN into a family with a lot of issues and managed to generate a few of my own, too.

Without going into excruciating detail: my family tree is abundant with alcoholism and other addictions, depression, and economic instability. There were a lot of "adverse childhood experiences"[1] in my life and in my parents' lives before me. I entered adulthood with poor kid syndrome, daddy issues, mommy issues, religious trauma, and a robust case of codependence. My compass was set to get approval from others, avoid disapproval, and the need to control everyone's thoughts and feelings and actions for my own safety.

In short: I was searching for the love, attention, and security that wasn't there when I was a kid.

I poured this into my writing, and it's part of what helped me succeed once I finally got published. I was able to draw from my wounds and my needs and my attempts to process my parental issues in order to give my coming-of-age novels the emotional depth that has since become my brand.

That sounds like a positive; in some ways it was and is.

But writing about it didn't fix it. My particular emotional damage got worse and worse even as my books got more successful. The only thing was I didn't *realize* I was getting worse because those external sources of love and approval via my author persona were really putting out. I got a lot of positive attention in what I think of as the "first wave" of my career, and for a while that covered over the gaping hole inside me where self-love and identity should have gone.

Around 2013, a series of choices driven by all my unresolved childhood stuff came to a head, and I hit an acute breaking point. I went into a kind of recovery process and began to build a healthy self-concept that was centered internally, not externally.

That was great for me.

And bad for my career.

I realized that a major driving force behind my writing career was my need for love and approval. I was building up a self-concept on the scaffolding of "author Sara Zarr." Maybe you relate to this. A lot of artists do. Then, as I worked on my issues and built myself back up from within, I didn't need that scaffolding. It fell away. Or kind of collapsed, really. It was a hard time in my career. I changed publishers, had an unusual-for-me gap between books, and found that as I grew less and less interested in pleasing others, they were . . . less pleased with me. Funny how that works!

So it was "bad" for my writing in that I started to question why I was doing it at all. Was it because I had to tell these stories in my brain? Or was it to get the attention I couldn't get from my father before he died? Was writing how I related to the world, or was it how I could feel okay about myself and the space I take up on the planet? My productivity slowed down and career decisions became more difficult. Though I was no longer acting to please others, I still wasn't sure what pleased myself.

In a lot of ways, I'm still in this phase of my writing life (and my life-life).

Rather than looking for some big answer, I've come down for now on the side of: this is my job. I'm pretty good at it and I have lots of experience to share in the contexts of teaching and mentoring as well as writing. Enough people are still interested in my books. There's not some other job I want. That's more than a lot of people get out of a career, and I can appreciate it on just that level even if "author Sara Zarr" is no longer the powerful, externally-sanctioned identity for me it once was.

"Being an author" didn't fix my childhood. But writing about it *has* helped me.

Few of my books are closely autobiographical, but all of them have some kind of family dysfunction, or include versions of other human-to-human experiences that have impacted me in some way. Putting those experiences into characters and processing them through their stories has done some inner repair work. I think the way this works for me is that telling a story about a hurt or an experience transforms it. I can travel back in time, *stop* time, go into moments that were painful and find the life or truth there. I can, as John Gardner put it, "design visions worth making fact." Even if I can't find a redemption tale in an experience, writing about it helps me let it go.

And then, in a story, it goes out into the world where maybe it will help someone else process *their* pain, or at least see it acknowledged, see it reflected.

The word "catharsis" gets thrown around a lot, to the point it loses some meaning. But the origin of that word is pretty interesting. It has a deep history involving Plato and Aristotle and war and society and trauma. It's enough to ponder here that the Greek word can mean purification, cleansing, or clarification. I experience all those things in writing my novels.

Of course, there's lots of space in the grand hall of writers for people to write lighter fare and not be trying to cleanse or clarify anything. People write and read for all sorts of reasons, and the motives of entertainment and escape are not lesser than those of catharsis and meaning-making.

Whatever you write, and for whatever reasons, it

might still be worth looking at your identity as writer and see if you're asking it to carry more than it can. Even the most successful career can't replace parental love, erase trauma, or be your whole identity.

---

1. https://www.cdc.gov/violenceprevention/aces/

21 /
bad days

WE ALL HAVE THEM. For me, bad days look like:

I can't stop cycling through apps and get to work. Distractions and to-do lists are winning, and I believe all my excuses. Or I get to work and I can't see what to do next in my book, how to start a revision, or any sign that my work in progress isn't garbage and that this whole endeavor isn't pointless.

Honestly, I have these days pretty regularly. Two decades of experience haven't fixed me or led me to a perfect process. I'm just one of those writers who struggles to get writing. My habit of sitting down to the Internet in the morning—as though "being on the Internet" is my primary job description—really does not help.

It's about more than changing habits, though. There are reasons we resist getting started, and they can be complicated. Our minds may be swimming in self-judgment, discouraging messages from childhood, or fears we haven't yet even identified. We may be thinking about unmet goals, unrealized potential, how we measure up to what we think being a writer should feel like. We get trapped in thoughts about the past and the future without ever seeming to get rooted in now. Being successfully published only seems to add to the inner noise rather than silencing it.

Sometimes bad days turn into bad weeks, bad months, or bad seasons.

What to do?

There's no way around it—these days, weeks, or seasons feel awful. We would like to avoid them entirely if we could. When it happens to me, I'm plagued by the sense that time is gushing down the drain. And lost time is lost words, lost progress, and frankly, lost or delayed money.

Which puts us back to the conundrum outlined elsewhere in this book, with regards to capitalism and the marketplace and the cultural norms that surround us. To wit: productivity is always good and not producing is always bad. It's commendable to challenge that thinking, but if you do happen to find yourself in the profession of "working writer," the relationship between productivity and survival is not abstract.

As someone who makes my living from writing and writing-adjacent work, I'm very susceptible to money anxiety when I'm having bad days. I look back at stretches of time when I got little writing done and wonder—what the hell was I even doing? I should have a draft by now! Look at Writer Friend A, who is writing at a pace I've only imagined. Look at Writer Friend B, who gets paid enough per book to not rush or feel the hounds of failure nipping at her heels. Look at Writer Friend C who has no online presence and yet sells tons of books. Why can't I be A, B, or C? Why do I have to be G or F over here, always struggling?

I spiral into comparison, shame, anxiety, and resentment. And—surprise, surprise—that stuff doesn't really help get me in the writing *mood*.

One thing I know: most writers experience this. No, I can't promise you that every single writer in all of history has felt this way, but I've talked to many, many writers and I can report that most feel *some* version of this, *some* of the time. Aside from the writers I've personally talked to, you can see it there in the biographies and collections of writers' letters, and in our modern-day version of that—tweets and blogs and other social media posts.

Knowing that makes me feel a little better, but it doesn't solve my problems.

As to the money part of it all, I'll repeat what I wrote in the last section: if putting financial pressure on your writing is sapping away your joy in the process, find some other way to make money or supplement your income. That might look like a full-blown non-writing career, or like Instacarting on the days you can tell writing is not going to happen, or something in between.

Do what you need to do to make writing financially and mentally possible.

And for the creative struggle on bad days?

Sometimes it's a "butt in chair" problem, and though I'm not fond of that phrase, it can be as simple as that. Break the cycle of scrolling, use an app to keep you offline, set a timer and commit to giving your brain at least fifteen minutes to shift gears into creative mode, or whatever version of "just do it" works for you.

Sometimes that's not the issue, though, and there's no glory in sitting there trying to scrape around in your creative well when it's dry. Hustle and grind language has worked its way in to how a lot of us talk about writing. We hear (or say) stuff like: get your word count in no matter what, write every day or you're not a real writer, man up, put your big-girl panties on, ship it, do it, crush it, no excuses. I . . . really hate this kind of talk.

If hustling only leads you to a dead end of exhaustion and burnout, it's time to do the opposite. Stop the grind. Stop hustling. Instead, get your butt *out* of the chair and look away from your work. Arrest the grind cycle and get centered back in your own mind and body. Breathe, walk, listen to music, do the dishes, run an errand, read something great, stare into space.

On my bad days, in my bad weeks—when staring at my manuscript real hard isn't doing it—I have to not only turn off distractions, but also turn my attention to something else. Something that's not my own work or ego. Productivity doesn't solve the problem. Performing online doesn't solve the problem. I need to give myself a chance to be pulled back into the work, and often that means stepping away from beliefs about productivity and getting in touch with the lofty, woo-woo ideals of the life of the mind.

22 /
mission statements & manifestos

I'M a mentor in an MFA program, and right now I've got two graduating students to whom I've given the following assignment: write your manifesto. Something about that word made them laugh, so I started calling it a mission statement instead. I like "manifesto"—it sounds grandiose and a little unbalanced. But mission statement will do.

I think all writers can benefit from doing this periodically. To me, it's more than a "why I write" statement. It's a "what I care about," that could even apply to choices you make outside of your writing life.

Mine has taken, oh, fifteen or so years to hammer out; there's no rush. It turned out I couldn't put it all together until I came across this quote from writer Iris Murdoch:

> "Love is the extremely difficult realization that something other than oneself is real. Love, and so art and morals, is the discovery of reality."

Murdoch wrote those lines in her 1959 *Chicago Review* essay, "The Sublime and the Good."[1]

As someone who has (thus far) mostly written coming of age stories, the quote immediately struck me as deeply insightful and connected at the very root to the coming-of-age arc. I don't just mean in fiction, but in my own life as someone who sometimes still feels like I'm coming of age.

What better describes the process of growing up than "the discovery of reality"? And what's more challenging as we learn to really love others than accepting that their lives are as real for them as ours are for us? The quote retroactively strikes me as the thesis statement of all my novels, as the families at the center of my stories try and fail to love one another and themselves in the face of difficult truths.

When we're children, our parents or caretakers are at least part a projection of our needs. That's natural and normal. Whether we have great parents or acutely flawed ones, giving and receiving love to and from them is necessary for our physical and emotional survival. As we move through adolescence, we start to see our parents or caretakers as who they actually are. The good and the bad, whether they disappoint or come through, their foibles and fears. Even the recognition that they *exist* in their own lives when we're not watching can be disorienting.

In adulthood, we keep doing this to greater or lesser degrees, depending on our upbringing. That is, we project. We struggle to see others as real. We want them to be who *we* think they should be, instead of loving or at least accepting the reality of them. Adolescence is where this work begins in earnest, and is at the very heart of what it means to come of age.

Is what we call "love" the experience of people being who we want them to be and meeting our needs and expectations? Or is it accepting those closest to us in spite of their limitations and mistakes? Does the latter type of love have its limits and, if so, where are those limits?

The context of Murdoch's quote is an essay attempting to answer the question, "What is art?" She's joining Tolstoy, Kant, and others in an ongoing conversation around this question, and for her, love and art and morality are all bound together in this issue of reality in a broader sense.

Pondering this helped me boil down my manifesto to something like this:

My allegiance in writing has always been to reality—which I don't mean in a genre sense, as fantastical stories can have an allegiance to truth and realism can be false. What I mean is that I try to see things as they are and write about them from that clarity of vision. Murdoch writes, "We may fail to see the individual because we are completely enclosed in a fantasy world of our own into which we try to draw things from outside, not grasping their reality and independence, making them into dream objects of our own. . . . Love [is] an exercise of the imagination."

I want to use my imagination to get outside my own

wishes and projections and not bend others (real people or my characters) to the will of my comfort, anxiety, or childish fantasies. Like everyone who wants to grow up, I have to press against the ways I wish people (and life, and stories) would just be who and what I want them to be instead of who and what they are.

That's my manifesto, my mission statement. That's what it is for now, anyway, though I want to always leave space for it to grow and change.

What's yours?

———————————————

1. https://www.jstor.org/stable/25293537

23 /
gratitude: a stay against bitterness

THERE ARE SO many things to legitimately complain about in the writing life.

Writing is hard, publishing is unfair, few of us make enough money to get by, books fall through the cracks, writing goes unappreciated, reviewers misunderstand us, we're misread on social media, the algorithm hates us, life conspires to keep us from writing, good books tank, bad books make millions, we get tired of our brand, sick of our niche, editors leave, computers die, our star may rise only to quickly fall, our star may be stuck under the radar, we don't get a movie deal, we don't get an audiobook, our editor is slow, there's a pandemic that delays our plans, our panel doesn't get picked, the conference invite doesn't come, our agent ghosted us, we can't even get an agent so they *can* ghost us, and did I mention that writing is hard?

I'm a firm believer that complaints are allowed. There *is* such a thing as toxic positivity, and women especially are conditioned to comply with it. We all need space to vent—ideally, to people who get it. This is what private text threads and Slacks and Zooms are for. Vent, bitch, complain, cry, whine. Get it off your chest so you can move on.

But/and I also know that gratitude is so important. It's the most effective tool we have against bitterness, and bitterness is an absolute creativity-killer. Bitterness is the state of constantly being stuck on everything you don't have, hanging on to every petty and not-so-petty gripe, holding grudges against people you don't even know for having something you want. It's hate-reading and hate-watching and hate-scrolling. It's "I get no respect" and "Don't they know who I am" and "It should have been me." It's the poison you drink yourself.

Complaints are a limited-time visit with our umbrage and grievances (which are often losses that we're sad about and maybe need to actually *grieve*, as the word suggests).

Bitterness is inviting them in to stay.

In my experience, being in mid-career (or midlife) is a time when we're especially susceptible to bitterness. As I become ever-more conscious of how much time I have left, I can get caught ruminating on all that I haven't gotten. Career milestone that may have passed me by. Missed opportunities and time I'd like to snatch back from people and situations that took it. The chance to be an "under thirty-five" sensation. (I was first published at thirty-six, and truly never had that chance!)

I went through a very bad phase of bitterness eight or nine years ago when it started to dawn on me that my popularity may have peaked. I had about five books out and now there was a whole new crop of writers. The marketplace changed and was less favorable to what I do. People move on to the next thing, as they do, and I was just really mad about it. I realized that somewhere along the way, I'd gotten so used to a certain amount of attention that I felt entitled to it.

That feeling of being entitled to something should be a red flag to ourselves.

For one thing, writers aren't entitled to much. We're entitled to be paid a contractually agreed upon amount and treated decently as humans, and that's about it! We're not entitled to readers, to be liked, to awards, to good reviews, to making lists, to conference invites, to movie options, more book contracts, or anything else.

For another thing, the second we feel entitled to something, we're setting ourselves up for bitterness, which is only going to hurt us and not solve any of the circumstances that may be in play as far as *why* we're not getting the things we feel entitled to.

Gratitude is the antidote. Not in a blind live-laugh-love kind of way, but in reflective acknowledgement of good things we have—from food, clothing, and shelter to people we love, to pets to hold. From clean water to a new story idea we're excited about. From the ways we've been saved from ourselves, somehow, to the chances we've had to lend our ear or shoulder to another. Maybe there have been some good career things along the way, too, that we've let grow insignificant in our memories because what we want is so much more.

Gratitude frees us from bitterness, which also frees us to engage in creative problem-solving (or in seeking justice, if that's what's needed).

If you feel yourself veering off into a place where your complaints are becoming more and more frequent and intense, and entitlement is creeping in and turning into bitterness, you might want to establish a gratitude practice. Some people write down three things they're grateful for, every day, or make it a weekly exercise, or just generally try to stay in that mindset.

For me, the gratitude mindset has been transformative. When I'm tripping up on bitterness or the thinking that leads to it, I try to gently redirect. What am I really feeling, how can I acknowledge it, what can I do about it, and what am I thankful for? The part of me that loves to hate woo-woo stuff hates the fact that this really works.

24 /
revisioning

I WAS an obsessive follower of women's figure skating in the 1990s. Kristi Yamaguchi, Tonya Harding, Nancy Kerrigan . . . maybe you remember. In the later part of that era, Michelle Kwan became my favorite. She dominated almost all competitions but could never quite get Olympic gold. Watching her try to make it happen was incredibly dramatic—full of pathos and suspense. There have been other athletes in her situation, as individuals or in teams. The high visibility of these "right now or never" competitions is far from the reality of the writing life, but they make for striking metaphors.

Maybe "the gold" for you is finally finishing a draft of a novel that's been hounding you for years. Maybe it's finding an agent who believes in your work, and then finding an editor who understands your vision. Maybe it's writing a *New York Times* bestseller or getting a Newbery Medal, a National Book Award, a MacArthur "genius" grant.

Maybe it's like mine—that I'll be able to keep doing this in the professional realm until I can't or don't want to write anymore. That's the gold I'm chasing now.

It wasn't always that, and it's still not exclusively that. I have lots of career milestones on my bucket list that I may or may not get to check off, depending on whatever alchemy of work, luck, skill, and persistence comes together. I used to be more ambitious, I think, believing that I had to prove something by continually one-upping myself. In skating, standard double jumps became triples and combos, and now everyone has to have a quad. I can feel that way sometimes about writing and publishing success. Is anything less than bestsellerdom and a movie franchise and a mansion next door to my nemesis James Patterson even "success"?

One of the gifts of being in this for half my life now is that I get to see the overstory. Not only mine (so far), but others', too. I've seen friends who thought their careers had peaked long ago go on to win major awards. I've seen superstars disappear (for now?). I've seen writers who started as unappreciated also-rans sit on bestseller lists for weeks upon weeks. I've seen some strivers settle into good, sustainable careers and others self-sabotage or get pushed out. Downfalls, comebacks, breakdowns, hiatuses . . . it all seems to be part of the deal.

You never know what's going to happen in a writing career, if a career is what you want. I don't know what's going to happen for me down the road, or for you, or for whoever is at the top of their game now, or for whoever seems to have flamed out.

I don't know if things will go as planned or desired for you, or for me.

I *do* know that the writing life—or the life of the mind, as defined at the beginning of this book—can be forever, if you want it to be. I do. It's how I make meaning, it's how I hold onto my belief that there's something bigger here, something more than meets the eye. It's how I stay out of bitterness and cynicism; it's a shield against despair. When I'm not living from the framework of the writing life, I don't feel like me. What I do feel, I don't like. The writing life keeps me in a continual act of creation, not just in the words I put down but in the way I experience being alive.

And the writing life is an act of revision as much as of creation. Anyone who has lived past the age of, oh, sixteen, has begun to understand that life is change. The older we get, the more this knowledge grows and deepens. We have to adjust our expectations and our thinking. The universe laughs at our plans. The world conspires against our goals. So we revise and resubmit. Maybe *this* is who I am. Maybe *this* is what I'll do.

The desire to write and create, and maybe to publish, will put us in an ongoing conversation with ourselves and with the world. The topics may change, the context may shift, but in this conversation, we get the chance to see and re-see and revise and remake our vision of who we are, what we want, and how we'll engage with the world.

This writing life, this creative life, is ours for the taking, and for the giving. For the receiving and re-envisioning and reshaping. And it never has to end.

epilogues

9 lessons from 100 conversations with writers

One hundred is a lowball guess. At the time of writing this, I've done seventy-nine regular interview episodes of the podcast, plus the Launch Box series. In my twenty years in the business I've also had dozens and dozens of informal conversations with writers at all stages of their writing lives. Certain themes come up again and again. I've addressed and expanded on many of them throughout the book. Here are many of them distilled in list form if you ever need a quick reminder that you're not alone.

1. Permission is a thing you give yourself. I can't recall a single writer I've talked to saying they waited for someone else to give them permission to do what they're doing. Some had a longer path than others to arrive at the moment they were able to give themselves permission, but ultimately—despite fears of being laughed at,

rejected, kicked out, told you can't do it—the permission has to come from within.

2. Learn-by-doing is legit. Though a fair number of writers I've talked to opted to get an MFA in Creative Writing or otherwise study their craft in a formal way, plenty of us (myself included) learned by doing. We wrote endless drafts, read a ton of books in the category we wanted to publish in, cobbled together ad-hoc critique groups, picked up a pen and notebook or laptop and jumped in. And speaking of permission, though a degree or workshop acceptance can certainly give you a confidence boost and help you learn more quickly, if you're waiting to be legitimized by these things, you haven't yet fully given yourself permission.

3. Most of us do better with some kind of routine. Whether it's something as loose as "write five days a week" or as detailed as "write from 8 a.m. to noon, break for lunch, walk, answer emails from 2 to 4, then write another hour," most people I've talked to try to have at least some sort of guideline for how and when they work. This doesn't mean we all stick to those guidelines perfectly. There's plenty of failure along the way, even among the most successful writers I know. That said, a schedule seems to yield better results than utter chaos, and consistency is key.

4. Most of us experience some degree of imposter syndrome. Yes, even the best-selling writers. Yes, even the ones with awards. Yes, even the ones on a ten-city book tour. Imposter syndrome is no respecter of persons! Many of us are perfectionists and fear we're not enough, or do our work with the fear that this time, we won't be able to do it. This time, everyone is going to figure out we're frauds. How do we get through that feeling? Talking about it, laughing about it, and not giving it too much power. It probably won't ever totally go away, but we don't have to give it free room and board.

5. Social media is a great and terrible thing for an artist. Most writers I know are into at least one of the triumvirate of Facebook, Twitter, and Instagram. (And, increasingly, TikTok.) Between books and appearances, these platforms can be the best way to stay in touch with colleagues, peers, and friends, as well as readers. We don't want people to forget we have work out there available to purchase or get from the library. At the same time, the platforms are rife with potential problems. "Comparison is the thief of joy," said . . . probably Teddy Roosevelt, possibly Mark Twain. This is true.

Comparison can also be the thief of productivity and confidence, and it's definitely the thief of time. Many of us struggle to not feel envy and bitterness when we see other writers seemingly getting something we want. Or we can start getting a scarcity mindset and fear there's not enough room for us at the table. There's always someone with a better book deal, better sales, a movie option, more followers, more likes, more awards, more conference invites. A few writers I've talked to over the years have no trouble turning this stuff off when they need to, but for most of us it's an ongoing tug-of-war to find a balance that works for us and not against us. If you can't find the balance, it's okay to ditch social media entirely.

6. Many of us have or have had struggles with mental and emotional health. But there is hope. Anxiety, depression, family of origin stuff, low self-esteem, and other issues are not uncommon among artists. On the whole, the writers I've talked to have found that leaning into self-care and, if necessary, medication, makes continued creativity possible. No productive working artist I know has found that life and career are better if they constantly live on the emotional edge or engage in sustained self-destructive patterns. The idea that art is helped by being emotionally unhealthy is outdated and harmful.

7. All of us have experienced career disappointments. I've been around long enough to see writers who were once at the center of every conversation slip into relative obscurity, and writers who'd all but thought their careers were over make a resurgence. Comebacks, reinventions, breaks, and reassessments are all part of any career that lasts more than a few years. The big wins are not a sign you'll never struggle again; the down times aren't a sign of eternal career doom. Finding a way to cope practically

and emotionally with the ups and downs is part of sustaining this for the long haul.

8. Some of us do better with a day job. Relying on your art for your living (and health insurance) can be very stressful, even when you're at the peak of success. There's a myth out there that you're not "really" a successful writer or artist until you don't have to do anything else for money. In truth, the majority of successful working writers I know are also teaching, speaking, and/or consulting; are married to someone with a regular paycheck and health insurance; or have kept other day jobs. And honestly? The job-having people I know are among the least angsty about their writing careers.

9. The happiest of us are in touch with gratitude. Gratitude is easy to write off as the fodder of fridge-magnet wisdom and lifestyle blogging, but it has real power. That's why it has its own whole chapter in this book! Being in a successful creative career is a function of hard work and skill, yes, but also a whole bunch of other things we can't control: timing, zeitgeist, current events, decisions made in corporate boardrooms—not to mention deeply entrenched systemic problems in the industry. Throwing out the myth that creative success is merit-based will help keep us in touch with humility and gratitude, and this makes us happier, better, more generous people, doing our best work both on and off the page.

11 lessons from 15 years in book publishing

As with the preceding list, this is a distillation of ideas I've expanded on in previous chapters, a handy go-to set of key reminders when it comes to the business end of being a writer. Most of these apply to life in the traditional publishing, as that's been where my experience is. Indie authors can extrapolate to their particular context.

1. The publishing business doesn't owe you anything. It's a business. If you start feeling like it owes you or it cares about you or it has a personal relationship with you, you're cooked. Why? For one, a sense of entitlement is personal and career poison. When you feel entitled to things, you stop working for them or appreciating the luck involved in getting you where you are. And for another, expecting love and loyalty from multinational conglomerates is one of the many roads to bitterness. Speaking of which:

2. Bitterness is a career-killer. (Can you tell by now that I'm *really* trying to drive home this point about bitterness?) Bitterness is the enemy of creativity and hope. Bitterness is when you take your eyes off your own paper and start looking at what others are doing and getting, fixating on how you feel wronged, obsessing over why you're better than x author who gets all the good gigs, nursing grudges, and spending more time editing your list of nemeses than editing your novel. (Can you tell by now that I'm *really* trying to drive home this point about bitterness?)

3. Invest in a few core relationships. I used to say things like "the writing community is great" or "I love the YA community," but "the community" is just a collection of individual people, some of whom are great and some of whom, frankly, suck. Always remember that the "writing community" isn't a monolith and it has its unpleasant corners as well as its lovely ones. You aren't going to be friends with everyone; that's okay. There will be people you actively dislike. That's okay, too. Find your core group of folks you trust and respect, and invest in those relationships.

4. Try not to be a climber. It may be that the core group that you trust and respect isn't the cool in-group of the moment. Life in publishing can be more than a little like high school. Who's in? Who's out? Who are you trying to get into your selfie for IG? Whose book cover are you

flashing to make sure they know you exist? You can easily find yourself trading in cultural capital and clout rather than seeing fellow authors as people and valuing them based on who they are vs. what they can do for you. A little of that is to be expected in any business, and to an extent it's part of building connections and tending to your career. Just try to be aware when you're doing it, and remember it's not the same as friendship.

5. Use your goodwill account carefully. If you're lucky enough to be in the business for a while and you're not an asshole, you'll accumulate some goodwill among editors, agents, colleagues, librarians, booksellers, and other publishing professionals. That's not nothing. Try not to squander it. I've made the mistake at various points in my career of tapping into that accumulated goodwill for things that weren't worth it, usually something that had to do with my own ego issues or insecurities.

6. But be generous! No, don't squander your career capital on being a diva or trying to feel important. But absolutely spend it freely on lifting up others. Be nice to new authors and writers who haven't made it yet. Always remember when you were that person. I've seen enough people in my time go through the cycle of being the wide-eyed newbie, then the new hot thing, then kind of slipping down the other side of that peak when the next new thing crowds you out. When you're on your way up, or you hold that spot for a while, don't

be a cliquish jerk. During the times when you happen to be on one of the downward slopes, you're going to meet some of the people you were a jerk to, now on their way up. And karma is, as they say, a bitch. They also say that what goes up must come down, and I've observed that to be true in publishing. Remember that, whether you're headed up or down or gliding along on a plateau.

7. A note to the "good" girls and boys, and you know who you are: there are few rewards in publishing for being a good little soldier. As I've already mentioned, do not expect loyalty from a giant corporation in return for yours. You can care about people and strive to work with the best ones you can, but where the rubber meets the road and you need to make decisions for your career, remember that your books are products. Your publisher did a Profit & Loss statement on your book before they ever acquired it. They may think you're the bees knees as a person, but if the bottom line isn't in your favor, your time is limited.

So be the squeaky wheel when you need to advocate for your book—a cover, a marketing plan, doable deadlines, a publication date that makes sense. Better yet, make sure your agent can be that person. You don't have to be an asshole, but sometimes you have to rock the boat. My personal ethic tells me that kindness and generosity are almost never a bad thing. If you feel the same, do it because that's you, not because you expect to be rewarded for it, and don't sacrifice what's best for you and your work on the altar of niceness.

8. For those of you with agents or who hope to someday have one: your literary agent is your true partner. As we've established, publishing companies are bottom-line businesses. They're corporate entities that may be sold off, acquired, moved, changed, merged, or folded. The editors and marketers and designers within them move around a lot, too. Your literary agent is the one person whose fortunes rise and fall right along with yours, so get yourself a good one. If the fit doesn't feel right, it's not right. I had one agent when I first started out who turned out not to be right for me. Firing her was tough, and I worried I'd never find another. But I did find another literary agent, and we've been happily partnered since 2005.

To me, what makes a good agent is someone interested in both short-term and long-term planning, who believes in open communication, has your back at all times without sugar-coating things, will tell you when your expectations are out of line with reality, can be tough without being a jerk, and is honest and available.

9. Learn how to let go. As products, physical books are subject to returns, bad reviews, overstock discounts, pulping, remaindering, and going out of print. When you're writing a book, it's mommy's precious baby. In pre-launch and launch, the publisher is excited. Shortly thereafter?

Any given season's books, including yours, can quickly become warehouse clutter. You can't let that mess with your head. A physical book's potentially limited lifecycle doesn't mean the book was a failure or a waste of time. It will live on in libraries and on shelves in homes around the world, and in the era of e-books, it can exist forever as a digital file. You've got to find value in the writing of the book, appreciate everything that happens for it as a product, and then let it go.

10. Sort out your identity. There are a couple of facets to this. One is to protect your identity as a writer. Note: I'm saying *writer*, not author. To me the distinction is this: *Writer* is me. It's who I am as well as what I do, and it informs how I see the world and go through life. *Author* is my job. I see "author Sara Zarr" almost as a different person than me-me. She's the public-facing part of my me-ness, but not the whole thing. The writer self is always with me and undergirds/overarches all of who I am, while the author self can be set aside and is only one part of who I am.

There was a time I did not make this distinction, and it got me into emotional and creative turmoil. When my career hit its first slump, I felt so miserable. (See: "Writing Won't Fix Your Childhood") I felt worthless and needy, while also entitled and resentful. Truly a terrible mix of feelings that were in danger of calcifying into—say it with me now!—bitterness. I learned through it that I need a life and interests apart from publishing and authoring so that I can protect that writer self from that poison.

11. Get the room service. If you're lucky enough to reach a point in your writing career where publishers are sending you to conferences or on tours and paying for your hotel stays, and you're doing the otherwise free labor of sitting in booths, being on panels, making nice with one and all, smiling and nodding until your head threatens to fall off, and meanwhile you are probably a flatlining introvert, don't agonize over whether or not the eighteen percent fee on an already overpriced room service burger is going to piss someone off. Order it, put on your pj's, and watch your favorite TV show. Tip generously, thank your higher power that you got this far, and enjoy every minute while it lasts!

keep the conversation going

If you want more of what you read here, the free This Creative Life newsletter means you'll get periodic posts about the writing life in your inbox, along with notification of new podcast episodes.

Is there a particular topic or question you'd like to see addressed in the This Creative Life newsletter, podcast, or follow-up books? Let me know using the contact form on the TCL site.

If readers of the paperback edition would like a clickable PDF of the recommended links and footnotes, that's also available. Find it all at

www.thiscreative.life

selected recommendations

An incomplete list of books, articles, podcasts, and films that I find helpful or inspiring in some way:

Books
Becoming a Writer - Dorothea Brande
On Writing - Stephen King
Bird by Bird - Anne Lamott
Naming the World - Bret Anthony Johnston
Craft in the Real World: Rethinking Fiction Writing and Workshopping - Matthew Salesses
Just Kids & The M Train - Patti Smith
The Habit of Being: Letters of Flannery O'Connor
Around the Writer's Block: Using Brain Science to Solve Writer's Resistance - Rosanne Bane

Articles/Sites
"Writers of Color Discussing Craft - An Invisible

Archive" https://www.de-canon.com/blog/2017/5/5/
writers-of-color-discussing-craft-an-invisible-archive
"How to Be a Writer" - Rebecca Solnit https://lithub.
com/how-to-be-a-writer-10-tips-from-rebecca-solnit/
"Against Technique" - Brett Lott https://
creativenonfiction.org/writing/against-technique-2/
"That Crafty Feeling" - Zadie Smith https://believermag.
com/that-crafty-feeling/

Podcasts

This Creative Life with Sara Zarr - The inspiration for
this book! http://www.sarazarr.com/podcast
First Draft and Track Changes - Sarah Enni https://
www.firstdraftpod.com/trackchanges
Waiting for Impact: A Dave Holmes Passion Project -
Dave Holmes - The connection may not be obvious at
first, but just trust me. This is about lifetime arcs in
creative fields, expectations, luck, going for it, and
growing up. https://www.exactlyrightmedia.com/
waiting-for-impact

Documentaries

Holbrook/Twain: An American Odyssey (2014) - What
if something you started doing in your twenties to pay the
bills takes over your entire creative life?
Toni Morrison: The Pieces I Am (2019)
The American Masters series from PBS https://www.
pbs.org/wnet/americanmasters/

acknowledgments

I'm grateful for all the writers on and off the podcast who have shared their experiences and thoughts about writing and publishing. I'm also grateful for every indie author who took the time to write a blog post, make a YouTube video, post to a message board, or produce a podcast that helped demystify the self-publishing process. I learned so much from you. Special thanks to my students and clients, and to Shelby Newsom. Thanks, as ever, to Michael Bourret, who is the only person who could have talked me out of this and didn't.

also by sara zarr

about the author

Sara Zarr is the acclaimed author of ten books (and counting). She's a National Book Award finalist and two-time Utah Book Award winner. She has served as a judge for the National Book Award and is a MacDowell Fellow.

(c) *Cat Palmer*

Sara's essays, creative nonfiction, and short fiction appear in *Image, Hunger Mountain online, Gather,* and *Relief Journal* as well as several anthologies. Her first book, *Story of a Girl,* was made into a 2017 television movie directed by Kyra Sedgwick. She is currently on the MFA faculty at Lesley University.

www.sarazarr.com

thiscreative.life

CPSIA information can be obtained
at www.ICGtesting.com
Printed in the USA
LVHW042354090522
718309LV00003B/636

9 780578 324104